# Mike Tyson

## The Complete Chronology

David Brown

# Contents

# INTRODUCTION

Mike Tyson is without a doubt one of the most iconic and controversial figures in the world of boxing. Known for his ferocious fighting style and tumultuous personal life, Tyson quickly rose to fame as the youngest heavyweight champion in history. From his early days growing up on the mean streets of Brownsville to his meteoric rise to stardom and subsequent fall from grace, this book will delve into the fascinating life and career of one of the most formidable and enigmatic athletes of all time.

Join us as we explore the chronological highs and lows of Mike Tyson's career and discover the man behind the legend.

# CHAPTER ONE (1966 - 1986)

Michael Gerard Tyson was born in Brooklyn, New York on the 30th of June 1966. Tyson had two older siblings - Rodney and Denise. Denise died of a heart attack in 1990 at the tender age of 24.

Tyson's mother was named Lorna. She is believed to have been a prostitute at one point. She died of cancer in 1982 before Tyson became a professional boxer. Mike Tyson later said that he barely knew his mother. Tyson would also say that not having a doting mother was probably vital for his boxing career. It toughened him up and made him independent.

Mike Tyson's biological father was a man named Purcell Tyson - about whom little is known. Purcell Tyson was said to be a cab driver of West Indian origin.

The closest thing Tyson had to a father was Lorna's partner Jimmy Kirkpatrick. However, Jimmy was never around and left soon after Mike Tyson was born. Mike Tyson described Jimmy Kirkpatrick as a street person. Someone who was always in a bar or pool hall.

Tyson's single parent mother had no husband and little money. Tyson remembers her as a person incapable of much affection.

Tyson's upbringing came on the streets of Bedford-Stuyvesant and Brownsville, the latter in particular a dangerous landscape littered with abandoned tenements. Tyson described the place he grew up as 'crime and drug infested'.

Tyson said he was a fat kid and had a lisp. The other kids used to laugh at him.

The young Tyson was called 'Fairy Boy' by the local kids and took to keeping pigeons. The lonely Tyson found solace in his pigeon coop and wished he could just fly away like his birds.

One day some boys attempted to bully Tyson and one of his pigeons was hurt. Tyson went berserk and beat the boy up. He would admit, many years later, that he loved the feeling, that he still relished the memory of it.

Tyson said that a big change in his life came when a friend showed him how easy it was to rob houses. Tyson tagged along and soon became an accomplished  thief. Tyson had rarely gone to school before but with the money he made from robbing houses he bought himself new clothes and turned at school more often.

At 12-years-old Mike Tyson was carrying a gun, mixed up with drugs and violence and running with the wrong crowd although - as he remembers - there was no other life available to people like him. Or so it seemed.

The future heavyweight boxing champion Riddick Bowe also grew up in Brownsville. Bowe said the young Tyson always carried a big bag of cookies around and was called 'Bummy Ike' by the local kids. Bowe said that Tyson was the sort of kid that you crossed the road to avoid.

Tyson's baby fat soon melted away in his early teens. By the age of thirteen he was capable of fighting most grown men - and winning too. He was incredibly strong for his age.

Stopped by the police in a random case of mistaken identity, the young Tyson had hundreds of dollars stuffed in his pocket from robberies which he cannot possibly explain. He is arrested. During a spell at Spoford Detention Centre, a visit to the Centre by Muhammad Ali inspires Tyson. He sees how much Ali is loved and respected and dreams of that attention.

Tyson ended up in a special upstate New York school, a detention facility called the Tryon School, where his colour and size, not to mention his stroppy moods, soon cause tensions.

By the age of 13, Mike Tyson had been arrested nearly 40 times.

Tyson took up boxing through up boxing through Bobby Stewart, a Tryon School staff member. Bobby Stewart was a former amateur and pro boxer. He was amazed by how strong Tyson was. Stewart said Tyson broke his nose with a jab.

Nearby to Tyron school lived the famous boxing trainer Cus D'Amato, now virtually retired and in his seventies. Bobby Stewart decided to take Tyson over to see Cus because he felt that as far as boxing went he had taught Tyson everything he knew.

Mike Tyson, though he became estranged from many, stayed in touch with Bobby Stewart. In 2013, Tyson had Stewart as an honoured guest at his one man show.

Cus D'Amato was an eccentric and wise boxing trainer who guided Floyd Patterson to the heavyweight championship and allegedly took on the Mob in the fifties (the real truth though was probably more complex). His rural Victorian house in the Catskills, which he shared with longtime 'companion' Camille Ewald, was like a dormitory for troubled youngsters attempting to become boxers or trainers.

The Catskill Mountains, often referred to simply as the Catskills, where Tyson lived with Cus D'Amato, are a mountain range in southeastern New York state. They are a popular destination for outdoor recreational activities like hiking, skiing, and fishing. The Catskills are also known for their picturesque scenery and quaint towns. It was certainly a culture shock for Tyson to go from Brownsville to living with white folks in the Catskills.

"That's the Heavyweight champion of the world," said Cus D'Amato after watching the teenage Tyson spar for the first time. Cus D'Amato became the father Tyson never had and legally adopted the youngster in 1981. Tyson was also close to Camille Ewald - who was Ukrainian.

Camille Ewald looked after the young boxers who trained at D'Amato's gym. She taught them to read and write and how to use cutlery. They were assigned chores around the house.
Tyson admitted that when he first arrived at D'Amato's house he considered robbing it. These basic criminal urges soon vanished.

Cus D'Amato's gym was above Catskill police station. Cus D'Amato had moved to the Catskills because he deemed New York too dangerous. D'Amato had not been liked by the New York mafia.

Cus D'Amato read Nietzsche and was an endlessly quotable eccentric and man of independent integrity. Norman Mailer described D'Amato as someone with 'The enthusiastic manner of a saint who is all work and no contemplation...a certain sort of very tough street kid one used to find in Brooklyn. They were sweet kids and rarely mean and they were fearless.'

Tyson, like all D'Amato's fighters, came to love his wise mentor and together they began a quest that would lead to the World Heavyweight Championship.

In contrast to other trainers D'Amato encouraged doubt and fear in his boxers. "Fear is natural. Fear is your friend. When a deer walks through the forest it has fear. This is nature's way of keeping the deer alert. Without fear we would not survive."

Cus D'Amato had been fairly forgotten and estranged from boxing for a long time when Mike Tyson turned up on his doorstep. Cus saw Tyson as his way to have the last word. In the twilight of his life he could confound everyone by suddenly producing another heavyweight champion.

Cus D'Amato was friends with businessmen Jim Jacobs and Bill Cayton, who owned the world's largest collection of boxing films. Jacobs and Cayton would become Tyson's managers when his professional boxing career began. Tyson was close to Jim Jacobs but not so close to Bill Cayton. Jacobs was funny and a good talker whereas Cayton was more reserved.

Mike Tyson later said there was always a slight air of mystery about Jacobs and Cayton. Both of them were vague about their backgrounds. Jim Jacobs had once shared an apartment with Cus D'Amato for ten years in New York. It was Jacobs who set up the training camps in the Catskills for Cus. There remain whispers in boxing that D'Amato and Jacobs were both secretly gay but these rumours were certainly never verified and so must be taken with a pinch of salt.

Bill Cayton began in advertising. He made his first million with hair cream (which might explain why his hair was always slicked back). After the advent of television, Cayton started collecting and restoring old fight films with a view to selling them to networks. Jim Jacobs was a boxing historian who was doing the same thing. The two men eventually found one another and joined forces.

According to Mike Tyson, Bill Cayton was the one with the money whereas Jim Jacobs was shrewd enough to latch onto someone like Cayton - who had more money and connections than him. Jim Jacobs was a great athlete in his youth and considered to be the greatest Handball player of his generation. He also owned the world's largest collection of comic books.

In 1978, Jacobs and Cayton bought the management contract of the great world light-welterweight champion Wilfred Benítez. Benítez would become a triple weight champion and fight Sugar Ray Leonard, Thomas Hearns, and Roberto Duran. Mike Tyson said that Wilfred Benítez visited the home where Cus lived and was basically like a child of limited intelligence trapped in the body of a boxer. Jacobs and Cayton would also later manage the lightweight champion Edwin Rosario.

As Tyson attracted attention as an amateur boxer, he continued to cause trouble outside the ring with alleged assaults and inappropriate sexual behaviour. Cus D'Amato and Jim Jacobs, aware of the fistic (and financial) potential of Tyson, kept him out of court and always minimised the fallout for Tyson. As a consequence, the young Tyson never faced the consequences of his actions or learned the difference between right and wrong.

The one person who did make a stand was Tyson's fearless amateur trainer Teddy Atlas - another D'Amato disciple. The furious Atlas pulled a gun on Tyson when he learned Tyson had made lewd sexual comments and advances to an eleven-year-old girl who happened to be Teddy's niece. Teddy Atlas was soon exiled from Cus D'Amato's home and gym - lest he should disrupt the carefully laid plans set down for Tyson. Atlas felt that Tyson was getting away with far too much and had to be confronted.

Tyson missed a spot in the American Olympic team because his all action style was better suited to the professional ranks. Tyson compiled a 24-3 record as an amateur.

A tall, clever and agile fighter could evade or even outpoint Tyson over three rounds in an amateur fight (though not many did) but avoiding him for ten or twelve rounds in a professional was a different kettle of fish altogether.

When Tyson was an amateur and fighting other teenagers, the trainers of his opponents sometimes wanted proof of Tyson's date of birth to confirm his age. He seemed so much stronger and bigger than kids his own age.

In 1983, a young amateur heavyweight named Lennox Lewis was preparing for the world junior championship and came to the Catskills in search of sparring partners. D'Amato put Tyson in the ring with Lewis and they sparred over four days. Lewis ended up with a fat lip and Tyson a cut mouth in these 'explosive' sparring sessions. Cus D'Amato predicted they would one day fight each other for the world heavyweight championship.

It is generally regarded that an Olympic Gold is crucial in establishing a superstar in American boxing (Ali, Sugar Ray Leonard, Oscar De La Hoya etc) but Tyson quickly became much more famous and marketable than Tyrell Biggs (the American boxer who had actually won heavyweight gold). In a sense Tyson bucked a trend.

Fighters with an all action style like Tyson are generally not suited to amateur boxing. It is in the longer format of professional boxing where this style becomes much more effective. The gloves are smaller, there are no headguards, and a fighter like Tyson has plenty of time to catch up with his opponent.

Tyson spends most of his spare time at this time either training or watching old fight films at D'Amato's house. It was not what you would describe as a normal life. D'Amato did not want to work Tyson's corner for poignant reasons. He didn't want Tyson to look over from the ring one day and see that he isn't there anymore.

Tyson was initially trained by Kevin Rooney. Rooney was a former welterweight boxer and disciple of the D'Amato stable. Kevin Rooney was a straight talking Irish-American with a self-deprecating sense of humour. He got on well with Tyson and they even shared a house for a time.

Rooney had replaced Teddy Atlas as Tyson's trainer in what could be described as difficult circumstances. It is perhaps not a great surprise then that Rooney and Atlas never had anything nice to say about one another in the years that followed.

Mike Tyson said that becoming a boxing prodigy and being constantly praised by D'Amato was intoxicating. The bullied little fat kid from Brownsville was now the bully. Tyson would occasionally sneak back to Brownsville - which was the last thing that Jacobs and Cayton wanted. They knew that they were sitting on a gold mine with Tyson. If they could keep him training and out of trouble he was going to make them millions.

Mike Tyson turned professional with a first round knockout of Hector Mercedes at the Plaza Convention Center, Albany, New York, on the 6th of March 1985. One month after Tyson's pro debut, Cus D'Amato died aged 77. Tyson was devastated by the death of D'Amato and a part of him dies too. Tyson claims later that boxing was no fun anymore. He had no one to please or make proud of him.

As far as Team Tyson goes, the most important person now is Jim Jacobs. Jacobs is much closer to Mike than Bill Cayton - though Cayton is the brains when it comes to business. Tyson is unlikely to fly the nest with Jim Jacobs around. If you watch the Tyson/Berbick fight notice the man in a suit who enters the ring straight afterwards and kisses Tyson on the lips. That's Jim Jacobs.

Tyson came to regard Camille Ewald to be his mother and looked after her long after Cus died. Camille was in her 90s when she passed away in 2001.

Tyson was small for a heavyweight (about 5'10) but what he lacked in height he made up for in width. He radiated strength and power and had the largest and most solid looking "shock absorber" neck (19 ½ inches). One is reminded of AJ Leibling describing another short heavyweight - the great Rocky Marciano. "He has big calves, forearms, wrists, and a neck so thick that it minimizes the span of his shoulders. He is neither tall nor heavy for a heavyweight, but gives the impression of bigness when you are close to him."

One of the main reasons why the young Tyson was so effective was speed. He had very fast hands and could put together devastating combinations. The young Tyson was also hard to hit. Tyson had been taught the "peek-a-boo" high glove defence by his mentor Cus D'Amato and also used to move his head a lot more when he was younger and so rarely presented a stationary target.

Most big punchers rely on one hand for their knockout punch. Tyson was rare in that he could punch equally hard with both hands. The young Mike Tyson was also one of the most intimidating fighters to ever step in a ring. Through his career one can plainly see instances where his opponents are terrified of him.

Despite the death of Cus D'Amato, Mike Tyson is soon pressed back into service. Trent Singleton, Don Halpin, Ricardo Spain, John Alderson, Larry Sims, Lorenzo Canady, Michael Johnson, Donnie Long, Robert Colay and Sterling Benjamin all became 1985 Tyson knockout victims with only Sims and Halpin lasting beyond two rounds.

Jim Jacobs and Bill Cayton sent tapes of Tyson's early fights to news stations and stills to newspapers and magazines. They marketed him brilliantly.

Mike Tyson wore black trunks and black boots with no socks in the ring as a tribute to old time fighters like Jack Dempsey. Tyson eschewed the traditional boxer's robe too and would simply come in with a towel over his torso.

Tyson looks invincible as a teenage boxing tearaway. His fights are over quickly in spectacular fashion and few boxers have ever had such presence in the ring. Tyson looks like some unstoppable primal force - almost as if he's Mr T in a Rocky montage rather than a real boxer.

Tyson rounded the year off with early kayo wins over Eddie Richardson, Conroy Nelson, Sammy Scaff and Mark Young. ABC pay $850,000 to put four of Tyson's upcoming fights on

Wide World of Sports. The bandwagon is starting to roll. The competition is modest but Tyson was already landing on boxing magazine covers before he'd even attained a world ranking or fought a fringe contender.

Tyson's early opponents were secretly chosen by the British manager and promoter Mickey Duff. Duff was a friend of Jim Jacobs. Duff had produced champions like John Conteh, Boza Edwards, Alan Minter, and Maurice Hope.

Tyson is kept busy with a constant schedule of fights. Jim Jacobs told the media that Tyson's busy schedule is a strategy based on the principle that practice makes perfect. Of course, keeping Tyson busy also lessens the chances of him getting into trouble - a fact Jacobs is well aware of.

1986 would be a fateful year for Mike Tyson as his level competition was stepped up as a title shot begins to become a distant thought for the first time. Dave Jaco is dispatched in the first and then a big white journeyman named Mike Jameson lasts into the fifth.

Fringe contender Jesse Ferguson (who later upset the Olympian Ray Mercer) takes Tyson into the sixth round in a bruising encounter. It is the first experience many boxing writers have of "Tyson Mania" at first hand and they come away impressed by the raw power of the young prodigy. Jim Jacobs was not amused though when Tyson made a silly comment about wanting to drive Jesse Ferguson's "nose bone into his brain" to the press. It's flippant (if somewhat dark) humour from Tyson but it doesn't help to project the marketable sort of image businessmen Jacobs and Cayton want their young charge to project.

The street kid in Tyson is always lurking barely concealed

beneath the surface however much money and fame he is managing to garner. This inner turmoil is controllable for now but it sometimes makes for a heady cocktail (even in the early days) when sluiced with the fistic arrogance that D'Amato drilled into him and encouraged.

Tyson's boxing hero was Roberto Duran - who was also prone to making outrageous statements about his opponents. Tyson was perhaps trying to emulate Duran with his bad taste comment after the Ferguson fight. Roberto Duran was one of the most revered and popular fighters in boxing history. The Panamanian icon established himself as one of the greatest Lightweight champions of all time in the seventies and then jumped two weight divisions to become the first man to beat Sugar Ray Leonard. He won world championships in four different weights and tangled with the likes of Leonard, Hearns, Hagler, Palomino, Cuevas, Buchanan and Barkley. When he fought the whole of Panama held its breath.

After a blowout of Steve Zouski, Mike Tyson's first major test came when he fought James "Quick" Tillis in May, 1986. Tillis was good enough to have fought Mike Weaver for the WBA world title in 1981 and was a stepping stone for many young prospects.

Tillis was crafty and durable and becomes the first person to extend Tyson the full ten rounds, ending Tyson's knockout streak. Quick Tillis is the first boxer to show that it is possible to frustrate and negate Tyson's blistering offensive and that - like all big punchers - Tyson was prone to frustration if his opponent was still there after a couple of rounds.

A dubious knockdown for Tyson costs Quick Tillis a draw on two cards. Tillis showed that Tyson was human - and even one-dimensional sometimes - if you were dogged and clever enough. Of course, Tillis did have the advantage of fighting a raw and inexperienced Tyson.

Tyson's next fight against Mitch "Blood" Green also lasted the full ten rounds and Tyson's marketability takes a slight stumble as a consequence. Mitch Green was from Tyson's neck of the woods and an unstable and eccentric character who used to be a street gang leader in his younger days. The pair will be forever entwined when they have a street brawl in Harlem in the early hours a few years later. That later encounter outside the ring joins the mounting evidence that Tyson is unravelling fast and not mentally equipped for fame.

Mitch Green was a huge heavyweight at 6'5 and used an octopus like grip to hold and frustrate the shorter Tyson in the ring. Green was never in any danger of winning the fight against Tyson but - like Tillis - he does present a blueprint of sorts for anyone looking to survive against the young dynamo.

Green had threatened to pull out of the Tyson fight when he learned he was only getting $30,000 compared to Tyson's $200,000. He only agreed to go through with the fight in return for being allowed to get out of his contract with Don King's son Carl King. Carl was basically a proxy for his father. Tyson was oblivious to this Don King related drama - though in hindsight he should have taken a few warnings.

Mitch Green demanded a rematch with Tyson - which would have been sellable after their street fight - but it never transpired. Green, a volatile and strange man, didn't fight for seven years after the Tyson bout and never became a contender again.

Eager to restore Tyson's image as a destroyer after two points decisions in a row, his handlers then threw him a couple of journeymen in the form of Reggie Gross and William Hosea. Both were dispatched by Tyson in the first round and, in June, 1986, Lorenzo Boyd is stopped in the second.

The following month Tyson was back in the ring for what appeared on paper at least to be a sterner test but is actually a shrewd choice of opponent - Marvis Frazier. Frazier is the son of the great former heavyweight champion Joe Frazier and Joe was also his manager, trainer, and generally everything.

Marvis was a decent heavyweight who was often in the top ten and capable of using his boxing skills (he was a world class amateur) to outbox bigger men but he was also small for a heavyweight and had none of his father's power or strength.

In 1983, Marvis was 10-0 with his best wins coming against the overweight James Broad and a faded Joe Bugner when he was thrown in against the formidable heavyweight champion Larry Holmes. Holmes stopped young Marvis in the first round, showing a palpable sense of distaste for his task. As Holmes batters the groggy Frazier on the ropes after the first knockdown one can clearly see Larry compassionately motioning for the referee to stop the fight.

Although Marvis had since repaired his career to a modest degree with several wins and some decent scalps in James "Bonecrusher" Smith and Quick Tillis, Tyson's management were certain that the younger Frazier lacked the physical strength or firepower to keep Tyson at bay. The press shared that analysis and criticised Joe Frazier for making the fight in the first place.

In what was arguably the most ferocious and devastating performance of Tyson's entire career, Marvis Frazier was stopped in 30 seconds of the first round, an uppercut leaving him helpless on the ropes where he slumped to the canvas. He never stood a chance of beating Tyson and Joe Frazier was lambasted for effectively sending his son out to be executed.

The spectacular win over Marvis Frazier meant that Tyson was hotter than ever. He was the natural heir to the Muhammad Ali/Sugar Ray Leonard throne as the sport's flagship star and money maker, someone who could transcend boxing. Tyson told ABC's Alex Wallau that he was ready to fight for the world title whenever his trainer and managers decided. Jim Jacobs told ABC that they were in negotiations with former champion Larry Holmes to fight Tyson.

Joe Frazier did not distinguish himself greatly after the fight between Tyson and Marvis. He said he smiled at the fate of Marvis because that's how he liked to see a man go out - on his shield so to speak. Marvis barely threw a punch so it wasn't exactly the most glorious defeat. Joe also got a lot of attention for his comments about Tyson after the fight and suggested that maybe he should be the one to test the young prospect! "I don't think the son of a bitch can hurt me."

Mike Tyson was dignified and mature after knocking out Marvis Frazier. You can see at the end of the fight he immediately rushes to Marvis with genuine concern and checks to see if he is ok. Tyson also maintained his dignity when asked about the trash talk that Frazier Sr has thrown his way. "I'd be a fool to get into an argument with Joe Frazier," said Tyson and leaves it at that.

After the Marvis Frazier fight, Tyson was quickly back in the ring against the huge Cuban heavyweight José Ribalta. Although Ribalta tended to lose his big fights he was a tough heavyweight capable of mixing in world class circles. He gave a spirited performance against Iron Mike and lasted into the tenth round before he was stopped.

There would be one more fight for Tyson before his title shot. Alfonso Ratliff was the former WBC cruiserweight champion and a decent test on paper although he had lost to Pinklon Thomas and Tim Witherspoon in his earlier forays into the deeper water of the heavyweight division. Ratliff tried to use his mobility to evade Tyson but was stopped in the second round, never recovering from the effects of a crunching left hand punch that deposited him on the seat of his trunks against the ropes.

Mike Tyson's world title shot was arranged for November, 1986, at the Hilton Hotel in Las Vegas. If he won he would be at 19 the youngest boxer to win a portion of the heavyweight championship.

The opponent for Tyson's first title shot was the Canadian based Jamaican WBC champion Trevor Berbick. Berbick was no mug and had upset the highly touted Pinklon Thomas to win the title. Berbick was though notoriously hot and cold and very beatable. Tyson's handlers would not have put him in with Pinklon Thomas so early but they had no such qualms with Berbick - who they saw as made to order for Tyson.

Tyson's nickname by now was 'Iron' Mike but he was often dubbed 'Kid Dynamite' in the boxing media. It is noticeable in fights of this era that Tyson has a nervous shoulder twitch - most apparent in the pre-fight build-up.

Although Berbick had lost three times to Bernardo Mercado, S.T Gordon and Renaldo Snipes, he was good enough on his day to have outpointed hot prospect Greg Page and gone the distance with Larry Holmes. Berbick was a strong, roughhouse (if somewhat crude) heavyweight and expected by many to give Tyson a test. The consensus in the boxing press was that if Tyson demolished Berbick he was the real deal because no one had demolished Berbick before.

One could discount Berbick's points win over Muhammad Ali in 1981. Ali was a shadow of his former self and had no business being in a boxing ring at that stage in his life. Those involved in making that fight should be forever ashamed.

Berbick had Muhammad Ali's old trainer Angelo Dundee working his corner and the camp exuded confidence in the preamble to hostilities. Dundee was born in Philadelphia in 1921 but wasn't really much of a boxer himself. He got into training fighters when his brother Chris became a big cheese on the Miami boxing scene through promoting. Dundee soon began to formulate his own theories about how to motivate and prepare his charges so that they were fully prepared for the ring. He worked with Carmen Basilio and the light-heavyweight Willie Pastrano before the young Cassius Clay entered his life.

Angelo Dundee's recent curriculum vitae had seen him working with the great Sugar Ray Leonard. He knew he had his work cut out trying to come up with a strategy that would negate Tyson's speed and power. Berbick spent two months training at Johnny Tocco's Ringside Gym in Los Angeles. The plan was for Berbick to box early, go to the body, and come on strong in the later rounds. Berbick, stupidly, ignored this plan when he got in the ring. Berbick had been irritated by press reports saying he couldn't take Tyson's power. It made him determined to meet Mike head on - which was a crazy strategy.

While a number of boxers were intimidated by Tyson and seemed to have lost before the bell had even rung (later Iron Mike victims Michael Spinks and Bruce Seldon in particular), Berbick was not phased by his task and even tried some kidology by insisting on wearing Tyson's signature black trunks and boots into the ring. Tyson always wore black in tribute to old time fighters but it was the champion's prerogative to choose colours so Tyson picked up a fine for his attire this night of nights.

Tyson later revealed that he was suffering from gonorrhoea but had been too embarrassed to see a doctor when he fought Berbick. Tyson also confessed that Muhammad Ali amusingly whispered "Get him for me" when introduced to him in the ring before the fight.

When the Tyson/Berbick fight began, Berbick was slain by the forces of his own bravado and Tyson's blistering speed and ferocious power. Berbick tried to maul, attack and hold his ground and paid the price.

After a rocky first round, the West Indian was demolished in the second, the finishing touch coming from a delayed reaction to a clubbing inside punch from Tyson as they wrested close. The punch shattered Berbick's sense of balance and took his legs away. It's still an extraordinary sight to see Berbick fall no less than three times from one punch.

The shellshocked Angelo Dundee was amazed by Tyson's handspeed at close quarter. The teenager seemed to be the real deal.

Boxing magazines declared the fight marked the beginning of the Tyson era and wondered who on earth could stop him. Tyson was compared to Marciano and Dempsey.

The boxer that Tyson came to identify with the most though was Charles 'Sonny' Liston - the former heavyweight champion. An ex-con, who was seemingly always in trouble, Liston was Mike Tyson before Mike Tyson - both in the ring and out of it. "Sonny Liston," said Tyson. "I identify with him the most. He wanted people to love him or respect him but it never happened."

# CHAPTER TWO (1987 - 1990)

Now that Tyson had claimed part of the title it was time to go after the other champions in the HBO heavyweight unification round robin that was under way under the tentacles of Don King. Tyson's toughest opponent was expected to be the savvy and teak tough WBA champion Tim Witherspoon. Many in boxing felt that if anyone could beat Tyson it would be Witherspoon although even "Terrible" Tim would start as a decided underdog given Tyson's rampant trouncing of the usually sturdy Berbick.

But late in 1986 Tim Witherspoon suffered a shocking loss when he was stopped in the first round by late substitute James "Bonecrusher" Smith - despite the fact that he had outpointed Smith in an earlier clash. Witherspoon seemed completely out of love with boxing in the fight, offering little resistance as Smith clubbed him with powerful right hands.

Witherspoon was embroiled in a growing dispute with promoter Don King and felt he was not getting the rewards his efforts had deserved. When Witherspoon had defended his heavyweight title against Frank Bruno in London in 1986 both men were contracted to receive around a million pounds. Witherspoon's share of his one million pound purse, after

King had deducted his fee and training expenses, was a paltry $90,000! Bruno ended up with several times more than Witherspoon despite being the challenger.

Witherspoon said Don King was so mean fighters were even charged for the food they ate at camp! If only Mike Tyson was taking heed of this. Witherspoon's passive surrender had revitalised Bonecrusher Smith's up and down career and he was now confirmed as Tyson's next opponent with the WBC and WBA titles on the line.

After losing his first professional fight to James Broad, Bonecrusher Smith had gone on an unbeaten streak which ended when he lost in the twelth round of a world title challenge to Larry Holmes. Smith could be frustratingly inconsistent despite his 6'4 frame and punching power. He knocked out British prospect Frank Bruno in the tenth round and former champion Mike Weaver in the first but dropped a decision to the light hitting Marvis Frazier and was handily outpointed by the talented Tony Tubbs.

The consensus was that Bonecrusher Smith's march 7, 1987, unification fight with Tyson in Las Vegas would be short but explosive. Whoever got their bombs in first would win. That common prediction proved to be completely wide of the mark. In the space of twelve tedious rounds, Smith went from Bonecrusher to "Bonehugger" as he wrapped the shorter Tyson in frequent embraces and held incessantly. Smith simply went into survival mode, content to last the distance losing every round rather than try and win the fight.

It was a frustrating night for Tyson and television audiences as the expected fireworks failed to appear - save perhaps for a moment in the last round when a right hand by Smith seemed to jolt Tyson for a moment. It was too little too late with

Smith losing by scores of 106-120, 107-119, and 107-119 on the judges' cards. Tyson's co-manager Jim Jacobs took his own revenge on the lacklustre nature of the fight by banning Bonecrusher Smith from appearing on Tyson undercards in the future.

1987 saw the release of the video game Mike Tyson's Punch Out!! It was developed by Nintendo and released for the NES. This game was a huge success and Tyson helped with the promotion. Tyson said it was a big thrill to have his name on a video game like this.

Although Tyson is now one of the most lucrative and talked about athletes in the world, 1987 seems to be the year when his personal life begins to fray and threaten his long term boxing success. There is an assault and battery charge and the first rumblings of discontent with his trainer Kevin Rooney.

Tyson is champ and incredibly wealthy but, somewhat lonely, is now seeking the perfect wife. Tyson's ultimate quest was to meet Cosby Show star Lisa Bonet. The enigmatic Bonet is apparently not interested though. This same year the 20 year-old Bonet would marry the singer Lenny Kravitz.

Tyson does manage to arrange a date with Head Of the Class star Robin Givens. Head of the Class is a popular American sitcom that aired from 1986 to 1991. The show follows a group of gifted high school students who are part of an honors program at the fictional Monroe High School in Manhattan. Robin Givens was 22 when Tyson her. She was privately educated and then studied as a pre-medical major while appearing in daytime soaps. Givens later claimed she dropped out of Harvard to be an actor but this was proven to be a false claim. Givens had made it up.

Robin Givens made her film debut in The Wiz when she was 14. The Wiz was a riff on The Wizard of Oz and starred Michael Jackson and Diana Ross. Givens was also a magazine fashion model as a teenager. Mike Tyson was surprised when Robin Givens arrived for their first date with her mother Ruth Roper in tow. Robin came as a duo - as Mike was to find out.

Tyson married Robin Givens on February 7, 1988, at Holy Angels Catholic Church in Chicago. They lived in a mansion in Bernardsville, New Jersey. Robin Givens was religious and articulate. She was though regarded with suspicion by Mike Tyson's managers.

Though they were careful not to say anything in public (at least initially), both Jim Jacobs and Bill Cayton privately thought that Robin Givens was a gold digger after Mike Tyson's money. In his autobiography many years later, Tyson said he once found Robin in bed with the actor Brad Pitt. Kevin Rooney also distrusted Robin Givens and her mother. "Robin Givens and her mother Ruth Roper stepped in and tried to grab all his money," said Rooney years later. "But, Jimmy Jacobs and Bill Cayton had tied all that money up where nobody could touch it, nobody but Mike."

Bill Cayton would later say that he and Jim Jacobs had never wanted to do any business with Don King. In fact, Cus D'Amato had told them both to avoid King. This created a problem because it would be impossible for Tyson to fight in HBO's unification tournament without doing business with King given that King controlled fighters like Bonecrusher Smith, Tony Tucker, and Pinklon Thomas. It was all but impossible to avoid Don King in the heavyweight division because he had most of the world ranked heavyweights under contract.

It was already obvious by now that Don King wanted to steal Mike Tyson from Jacobs and Cayton. A familiar underhand tactic of King in situations like this was to ask the black fighter why he had white managers taking a cut of his purses - as was the case with Tyson. It was gross hypocrisy from King because he had ripped off more black fighters than anyone alive. Bill Cayton would later say that Robin Givens was a 'phony' who got Mike to marry her by pretending to be pregnant. Cayton would blame Don King and Givens for turning Tyson against him.

Bill Cayton later said that he and Jim Jacobs had tried to avoid the HBO unification tournament with an alternative plan. They planned for Tyson to fight Larry Holmes and then Gerry Cooney - two fighters not affiliated to Don King. However this fell through when Holmes couldn't be pinned down on a deal. Jacobs and Cayton found they could control Don King at first because they controlled Tyson and this gave them power. Once the HBO tournament was over, Cayton and Jacobs planned to have Tyson fight as a free agent where a different promoter staged each event. Don King though was desperately trying to wedge himself in as Tyson's exclusive promoter.

Tyson is back in the ring in May 1987 to fight former champ Pinklon Thomas - who by now is somewhat faded thanks to battles with drugs. Thomas has a great jab and Angelo Dundee in his corner but Dundee goes 0-2 against Iron Mike when Thomas is stopped in the sixth by a blizzard of punches that could have felled a tall building. After a shaky first round Thomas had been doing fairly well negating Tyson's offensive thunder but once he got caught the end was inevitable.

The HBO tournament to unify the heavyweight championship (a unification tournament which Tyson was expected to win) had suffered a fork in the world when Michael Spinks was stripped of his IBF title for refusing to fight the number one contender Tony Tucker. The general assumption was that Tyson v Spinks would be the culmination of HBO's unification tournament. These plans were now ruined.

Spinks, a distinguished former light-heavyweight champion, had made history when he outpointed Larry Holmes for the heavyweight title in 1985. Spinks repeated the feat by outscoring Holmes in the rematch in 1986 - though most people thought Holmes won that second fight. Spinks was the linear champion (or "People's Champion" as his team preferred to say) but Spinks and his close friend and promoter Butch Lewis did not want television dictating who they should fight next.

Michael Spinks and Butch Lewis knew that for Michael, a blown up light-heavyweight now over thirty and with dodgy knees, it was now a question of getting the maximum amount of money for the least amount of risk in the time he had left. The thoughtful and reclusive Spinks was not someone who was going to end up like his brother Leon. He would happily retire and walk away when the time came. Spinks and Lewis turned their attention to a rusty but valuable antique by the name of Gerry Cooney.

Gerry Cooney, a 6'6 tall white heavyweight from New York, was once projected by his managers Mike Jones and Dennis Rappaport to become the world's first billion dollar athlete. A real life Rocky. The handsome and genial Cooney was boxing's poster boy in the early eighties and raced to a superfight with Larry Holmes in 1982. The fight turns out to be man against boy though as Holmes navigates Cooney's thunderous left-hooks to the body and stops the brave but exhausted challenger in the thirteenth round. Whereupon Cooney went into hibernation, fighting just five rounds in the next four years against the unthreatening trio of Phillip Brown, George Chaplin and Eddie Gregg. Carefully matched and frequently inactive, Cooney made millions of dollars from boxing because of his skin pigmentation. The fight between Spinks and Cooney was set for June 1987 in Atlantic City.

Despite his inactivity, Cooney was the slight favourite with oddsmakers because of his sheer size and vivid memories of that devastating left-hook. Surely he would be able to blast out a little fellow like Spinks once he had him trapped? But when the fight started Cooney fought like a man who had been embalmed. He was frozen and mechanical and seemed unable to pull the trigger on the left-hook the way he used to in the past.

Spinks had a look-see for a few rounds and then, realising that the lumbering giant in front of him was no threat at all, began to flash a powerful jab and tee-off on the big New Yorker. Cooney, like many big punchers, often looked bewildered and confused when someone actually had the temerity to start hitting him back and displayed a hopeless lack of defence as he was stopped in the fifth round, hitting the deck twice. It was mission accomplished for Butch Lewis and Spinks. Whatever his merits as a fighter by 1987, Cooney was a big name and now Spinks even had folks wondering if he might be the person who would hand Tyson his first defeat.

Conventional wisdom was that Butch Lewis and Spinks were terrified of Tyson. Now it was just possible that Jacobs and Cayton might be having second thoughts. The logic went something like this: if Quick Tillis can give Tyson fits then what about an even more intelligent and cunning pugilist like Michael Spinks - one of the greatest light-heavyweight champions of all time? Having navigated Cooney's bombs and thrown a few of his own, Spinks had given everyone something to think about.

The IBF belt that Spinks vacated was picked up by Tony Tucker when he stopped James "Buster" Douglas in the tenth round. It was a fight that neither man seemed especially desperate to win but Tucker came from behind to batter the talented but sometimes unmotivated Buster. It was now Tony Tucker who would fight Tyson in a bout which would finally give the world a unified heavyweight champion for the first time since the days of Ali.

Mike Tyson and Tony Tucker faced off on August the 1st 1987. The fight took place at the Las Vegas Hilton in Las Vegas, Nevada. The fight - the claims of Michael Spinks notwithstanding - would unify the alphabet belts and create a unified heavyweight champion. Tony Tucker was given no chance at all against Tyson despite his physical gifts. He was a huge heavyweight with good speed and mobility but his level of competition was modest and Tucker could hardly fail to be distracted by a ludicrously complicated promotional and managerial arrangement that saw countless figures in the world of boxing claiming a piece of him. Tucker would later claim that he lost interest in the Tyson fight during training because he knew he would more than likely walk away with little of his pay packet.

Tony Tucker, in red trunks, gave a better than expected account of himself at the Hilton Hotel, taking Tyson's best punches and even temporarily lifting Iron Mike off his feet with an uppercut in the first round. Tyson won handily on the scorecards but it was another reminder that he could have frustrating nights if his his opponent was durable and knew how to tie him up.

After the Tucker fight there was a garish ceremony where Don King gave Tyson a crown to celebrate becoming the 'king' of the division. Michael Spinks and Butch Lewis were spectators at the Tyson/Tucker fighter - sitting way back in the cheap seats. Oddly, Jacobs and Cayton were in no rush to make Tyson v Spinks. They were happy to let Spinks get a bit older and doubtless not looking forward to have to negotiate with Michael's shrewd promoter Butch Lewis.

Tyson's last engagement of 1987 was a bout with 1984 Olympic super heavyweight champion Tyrell Biggs. When the pair were amateurs it was speculated that Biggs and Tyson could be the Ali and Frazier of the eighties and nineties and forge a classic rivalry. While Tyson had been sensational as a pro and looked like an all time great in the making the same could not be said of Tyrell. Biggs had squandered his natural talent with drug problems and his professional career was unimpressive so far.

Biggs had appeared on the brink of defeat against the faded David Bey before rallying to a sixth round stoppage and some wondered (not unreasonably) if throwing him in against Tyson after only fifteen fights was his management (the Duva family) cashing in the payday while they still could. There was said to be bad blood between Tyson and Biggs and although Biggs denied this it was the case it was clear that Tyson didn't like him much and seem to harbour some sort of residual grudge from their amateur years.

The Tyson/Biggs fight took place in Atlantic City and Biggs - in white trunks - used his height and boxing ability to shade the first round. It was a fleeting reminder of how good Biggs might have been had drugs not wrecked his potential. Tyson soon took control and in what was regarded by many to be his greatest ever performance he battered and bullied the increasingly bloodied and helpless Biggs until the fight was ended in the seventh round. Tyson endeared himself to no one afterwards when he boasted that he could have ended it much earlier had he wanted to and that Biggs "cried like a woman" whenever he was hit to the body.

Tyson was given a few months off and then began 1988 with a fight against the great former champion Larry Holmes in Atlantic City. Holmes was 38 now and had been out of the ring for a couple of years. The thought of him taking on a devastating young slugger like Tyson made people think of Rocky Marciano having to batter a shot Joe Louis into submission.

Larry Holmes didn't have much time to train for the Tyson fight but he couldn't resist the $3 million payday on offer. It was Don King who secured Holmes for the fight - which was bad news for Jacobs and Cayton because it meant they would have to work with King again. Behind the scenes King was doing everything in his power to get in the ear of Tyson and turn him against his managers.

1988 was pretty much the high water mark for Mike Tyson as a fighter. He was devastating in this year and seemed unbeatable. 1988 was also the high water mark for Tyson as a public figure. At the time he was doing commercials and was (in what was darkly ironic in hindsight) a spokesperson for the Drug Enforcement Administration. Tyson was still a mainstream commodity. A role model even. He would eventually became a circus freak show - albeit a lucrative freak show.

One of Tyson's best friends was Steve Lott. Lott was the training camp co-ordinator for Tyson. Lott was part of the team that Cus D'Amato had put in place before his death. Lott would later say that the combination of Don King and Robin Givens ruined Tyson as a fighter. According to Lott, Don King would take Tyson to Cleveland and lay on women for him in an attempt to brainwash the troubled young boxer into switching his loyalty from Jacobs/Cayton.

Tyson's commercial deals at this time included Pepsi Cola, Nintendo Video, and Kodak Film. In the late 1980s he was the most famous athlete in the world.

Larry Holmes had made comments about fighting Tyson for a few years before their fight, declaring that he wasn't much impressed by the young champion. Was he merely angling for a payday or did he really think he had a chance? Tyson was respectful of Holmes and said that D'Amato had always taught him to be wary of great former champions because even in their twilight they were capable of one last hurrah. In his later biography, Tyson said that Cus D'Amato didn't like Larry Holmes and never rated him.

The night of the fight Holmes looked strangely skittish and apprehensive as he limited himself to stretching out a long left paw, trying to keep Tyson at arm's length and then tie up the shorter man. It worked to a degree but Holmes barely resembled the man who had once dominated the division. He appeared heavy around the midsection and his once potent left-jab was a shadow of its former self.

In the fourth Holmes got up on his toes and started flicking jabs as the crowd began to chant his name. A patient Tyson waited for an opening and then nailed Holmes with a crunching right-hand that deposited Larry on the canvas with an audible thud. Holmes was known for his amazing recuperative powers and somehow beat the count but he wasn't going to last much longer. The former champ tried to wind up an uppercut but got his arm caught in the rope. Tyson knocked him cold with a devastating volley and the fight was over.

Holmes later said he was there for the payday and never had enough time to train. "As I neared the ring," said Holmes. "I had this weird thought: Why not be the first fighter to refuse to go into the ring? All those people watching on HBO, I'll amaze them all." Every boxer seems to have an excuse after a loss but we can maybe cut Larry some slack this time. Holmes returned to boxing again in the 1990s in his forties and upset hot prospect Ray Mercer and extended Evander Holyfield the full twelve rounds in a 1992 heavyweight title fight. The Holmes who beat Mercer was unquestionably in much better condition than the one whacked out by Tyson.

With Holmes out of the way thoughts turned to Michael Spinks again. It was the fight that boxing wanted and the obvious Superfight for 1988. The intransigence of Butch Lewis demanding $15 million for Spinks was cited as the major obstacle although Tyson's management had hardly been easy to deal with themselves. In the end third parties were able to (metaphorically) knock some heads together, or put people in a room at least, and Butch Lewis finally signed an agreement for the bout to go ahead in June. Tyson would get $20 million and Spinks $13.5 million. All Tyson had to do first was beat Tony "TNT" Tubbs.

Tyson's wife Robin Givens was starting to get media attention at this point. Robin proved to have a good sense of humour and, as one might expect of an actor, was comfortable in front of a camera. She told the media that if they had a son it would be called Cus and that Mike planned to break Rocky Marciano's 49-0 record and then retire. Robin told the media that Tyson's toughest opponent was his mother-in-law.

The heavyweight championship - at least up until the days of Mike Tyson - had traditionally always been dominated by American boxers and so for obvious reasons of commerce and convenience championship bouts usually took place in the United States. Jacobs and Cayton liked the idea of Tyson rekindling the days of Muhammad Ali and undertaking a world tour of sorts. Ali would hit the road and defend his title in far flung places, from Zaire to the Far East to the great European cities. It made sense for Tyson to resurrect this tradition because he was hugely famous and people around the world were eager to see him in the flesh.

Tyson's proposed schedule was supposed to see him fight Frank Bruno in London, Francesco Damiani in Rome, and perhaps even Adilson Rodrigues in Rio but none of these foreign adventures occurred in the end. One of the main reasons why Jacobs and Cayton wanted to take Tyson on the road was to work with foreign promoters and thus cut Don King out their Tyson promotions. One foreign trip Tyson did undertake though was to Japan in March, 1988, to defend his belts against Tony Tubbs in Tokyo.

Thirty year-old Tony Tubbs was symbolic of the overweight underachiever era of eighties heavyweights that included the likes of Greg Page and Tim Witherspoon. All were very talented but seemed to spend more time at the breakfast table than the gym. Tony Tubbs was a brilliant amateur boxer and had done pretty well as a pro too but he was clearly carrying a bit too much weight. Tony would also have battles with cocaine in his life.

Tony Tubbs was supposed to be trained by Richie Giachetti, the former trainer of Larry Holmes, for the Tyson fight. Giachetti left Tubbs though because the fighter wasn't willing to buckle down to the tough training regime he had put in place. Like many heavyweights, Tony Tubbs had a troubled history with Don King. Tubbs had sued King after King left him out of the HBO unification round robin. However, Tony had dropped the lawsuit against King when King got him the Tyson fight.

Tubbs was chosen by the Japanese promoters to fight Tyson because his sheer girth and deft boxing skills were at least expected to vex Tyson for several rounds and give them value for money. That assumption proved to be completely wrong. Tubbs had only lost one fight before Tyson. That was a majority decision loss to Tim Witherspoon in 1986. this loss had cost Tony his WBA title.

Tyson was a big celebrity in Japan and even met famous sumo wrestlers before the fight. Despite the talent of Tony Tubbs, Tyson's camp didn't take him very seriously. Tony was a boxer rather than a puncher so Tyson would be able to go straight after him without fear of anything too thunderous coming back his way. Tubbs and his trainer Odelle Hadley were confident before the fight. Hadley told the media that if the fight went past five rounds then Tyson would lose. Sadly for Hadley and Tony Tubbs though the fight didn't go that far.

Like Tyrell Biggs, Tony Tubbs used his reach advantage and speed (Tubbs had fast hands for such a big man) to outbox Tyson in the opening round - although the round was shared on the judges' scorecards. Tubbs boxed well in the second too, again troubling Tyson with his speed. But Tyson was implacable as ever, biding his time while he waited for a chance to unload his heavy artillery. Tubbs' willingness to fight in close was his undoing. As the second round neared its end, Tyson landed a body-head right-hand combination and a woozy Tubbs was finished with a left-hook. The punch was so horrific that Tubbs' trainer immediately entered the ring to signify that he wouldn't let his stricken charge take any more punishment.

When Tyson returned home from Japan after the Tubbs fight he was shocked to learn that his co-manager and friend Jim Jacobs had died. Jacobs had not been in Japan for the Tubbs fight. It was the only Tyson fight that Jim Jacobs hadn't attended. Jacobs, who was 58, had been suffering from leukaemia for nine years but it had been kept secret from Tyson. Tyson had another bombshell when he learned that Jim Jacobs' stake in him now transfered to Jacobs' widow. This was the sort of stuff that Don King could use to get inside Tyson's head.

Jim Jacobs was inducted into the Handball Hall of Fame, International Jewish Sports Hall of Fame and the International Boxing Hall of Fame. He was laid to rest at Hillside Memorial Park, Los Angeles. It was Jim Jacobs who had the final say on Tyson's opponents and handled the media. He was going to leave a big hole in Team Tyson. Fate now left Bill Cayton the only man alive out of the trio that created and established Tyson. But Cayton, a cold fish according to the boxer, wasn't nearly as close to Tyson as Jacobs and D'Amato had been.

Bill Cayton would later dispute the perception that he wasn't close to Mike. He said Mike loved him and they spent a lot of time together. Bill Cayton said that one of his plans was to educate Mike Tyson about business. Cayton said that if Tyson understood business and finance then he would never be broke. The lucrative commercial deals that Tyson had were all done by Cayton. It was also Cayton who got Mike big money to fight in Japan. Bill Cayton was actually doing a good job for Tyson but Tyson couldn't seem to see that.

Not only did Cayton have Don King spinning against him but it soon became apparent that Tyson's wife Robin also disliked and distrusted Cayton. Cayton just couldn't win. The two people (King and Robin Givens) with the most influence over Tyson were both mounting a campaign to have him removed. At Jim Jacobs' funeral, Don King arrived like a vulture and gave Mike Tyson a limo ride. King knew that control of Tyson was essential to anyone looking to control heavyweight boxing.

The young Don King was a a petty criminal involved in gambling and a 'numbers racket' in his home city of Cleveland. He once shot and killed a man but got off on a case of self defence and justifiable homicide. He wasn't so fortunate when he kicked to death a gambler who owed him $600. He got four years in prison for manslaughter. In 1971 King listened to the first Ali v Frazier fight in his jail cell on a radio. Four years later he was personally promoting the third Ali v Frazier in Manila. In this case truth is stranger than fiction.

Don King got into boxing by accident really. When he was released from jail, King asked Muhammad's Ali's people if Ali would box an exhibition in Cleveland to raise money for the local hospital. Ali, generous soul that he is, agreed to support the charity event and went to Cleveland for the exhibition. King raised $86,000 from the event but Cleveland Hospital only got $5000 of it! That was the way King operated right from the start and the exhibition opened his eyes to the possibilities of boxing for a sharp man like him. There was a fortune waiting to be made in this shadowy business. He knew he was smarter than the people who controlled boxing and a great salesman.

Don King is encapsulated by a moment at the end of a contest between King's fighter Michael Dokes and a South African named Gerrie Coetzee in 1984. Dokes was counted out on the canvas late in the bout and lost his WBA heavyweight title. His abiding memory of the fight is lying groggily on the canvas trying to regain his senses and seeing his promoter and 'friend' Don King step over him to go and congratulate Coetzee! This was of course the secret of King's success. He did his utmost to leave with the winner.

Don King started promoting in Ohio on a small scale but he was incredibly ambitious and already scheming. King was fantastic at his job, a twisted genius who could sell ice to Eskimos. King was incredibly audacious in making his big break. He promised Ali and Foreman so much money to fight they couldn't turn turn it down. The only problem was that King didn't have any money. He persuaded the government of Zaire to stage the fight and became a big player in the world of boxing.

Mike Tyson's long awaited fight with Spinks took place in June 1988 at the Convention Hall, Atlantic City. It was the richest fight in history and both the live gate and television audiences around the world anticipated a classic encounter between two unbeaten champions (although Spinks had been stripped of his alphabet belt he was, lest we forget, the linear champion).

Tyson was a heavy betting favourite but there were plenty of experts and pundits making the case for Spinks. At the very least maybe he would play Billy Conn to Tyson's Joe Louis. The key player in attracting the Tyson v Spinks fight to Atlantic City was none other than Donald Trump - at the time a famous businessman rather than a divisive politician.

By this stage there clear tension between Tyson and his

trainer Kevin Rooney. The source of the tension was simple. Rooney hated Don King and made no secret of his disdain for the promoter. Tyson, who was being increasingly sucked into King's orbit by the manipulative promoter, didn't like Rooney's attitude. Kevin Rooney later said he had a 'handshake' deal to be Tyson's trainer for life. Unfortunately for Rooney, handshake deals don't count for very much in the cut-throat world of boxing.

Mike Tyson would, many years later, say he didn't cope with fame very well - but then who would? To suddenly be world famous and rich at 19 was an experience few could breeze through. Tyson said the worst thing was not knowing who your real friends were. Did people just like him for his money and fame?

In the dressing rooms before the big fight, Michael Spinks' promoter Butch Lewis, clad in a white tuxedo with no shirt, made what was obviously a big error when in his capacity as an observer he objected to a bump in Tyson's hand wrapping and caused a delay by insisting it be rewrapped. In the end it was Spinks' venerable trainer Eddie Futch who ended the nonsense by declaring he could see nothing wrong with the wrapping. Tyson was furious and paced around the room becoming more infuriated by the second. He told his trainer Kevin Rooney that Spinks was going to pay. Tyson was so angered by Butch Lewis before the Spinks fight he punched a hole in his dressing room. Imagine being Michael Spinks on the other side of the wall!

Michael Spinks did not exude confidence before the Tyson fight as he made the long walk to the ring in a white robe. He seemed to be talking but he looked distracted and unsure of himself. The journalists who had visited the training camp of Michael Spinks had come away with the impression that no one in the camp thought that Michael could really beat Tyson. It was a very gloomy atmosphere in that camp. Michael Spinks was plainly never that thrilled to be fighting Mike Tyson but he had choice because how could he turn down $13.5 million?

Tyson was Tyson. He looked all business and deadly serious. While Spinks looked dry and slightly paunchy at a career high 212, Tyson dripped with sweat and looked like a tank in human form. Spinks stared down when the boxers came together for their instructions, like a man heading for the firing squad. At the bell Spinks seemed to forget everything he'd ever learnt about boxing (which, needless to say, was a considerable amount). It was no secret that he was a notoriously slow starter while Tyson's record was awash with early knockouts. Spinks needed to fight the first round as if it was the fifth. He had to minimise contact and establish a jab. Was it fear that made him forget everything?

Spinks lumbered towards Tyson in clumsy fashion, initiating clinches (the last thing Futch wanted him to do because that would be a test of strength with only one winner) and throwing a few weak telegraphed right-hands that looked desperate. Tyson maneuvered him towards the ropes and landed a right to the body which made Spinks take a knee to regroup. It was the first time Spinks had been down as a professional boxer.

When the action resumed Tyson knocked Spinks unconscious with a right-uppercut and with only ninety seconds of the first round gone the contest was over. The Superfight had been the Superslaughter. The Spinks fight is now seen by many as the peak of Tyson's career. It was Tyson at his most destructive and unstoppable.

Tyson now appeared to be unstoppable with the world at his feet but chaos was about to envelop the increasingly troubled young boxer. He railed at the press after the Spinks fight and threatened to retire. At the Tyson-Spinks afterfight press conference some friction between Kevin Rooney and Don King is clearly noticeable. Rooney has words with King when King tries to get into Tyson's limelight. There can only be one winner in this power struggle and it assuredly won't be Rooney.

Tyson was supposed to fight Frank Bruno next in London but the fight is endlessly rescheduled as Iron Mike is in no condition to think about boxing. He will not fight again in 1988. Tyson now sued Bill Cayton to try and break free from his managerial contract. Cayton was handed the legal papers to dismiss him while he sat ringside at Tyson v Spinks.

Tyson's wife Robin Givens was portraying Bill Cayton in the media as a crook who was stealing Mike's money. According to Bill Cayton it was also Robin who persuaded Tyson to fire his friend Steve Lott at this time. Tyson was basically getting rid of the entire team who had developed him and made him rich. The great irony of this drama is that Bill Cayton had cut great deals for Tyson and was a very savvy businessman. Most experts contend that if Mike Tyson had stuck with Bill Cayton he wouldn't have ended up in such a financial mess - especially in matters of tax. Cayton would have put long term plans in place to give Tyson an income for life.

Bill Cayton eventually agrees to cut his one-third share of Tyson's earnings to 20% but the fighter has slipped from his grasp and the estrangement will not be repaired.

Their contract doesn't officially end until 1992 but Cayton is manager in name only until then. He is estranged from Tyson and has no say in Tyson's career anymore.

By now, Tyson's wife Robin Givens has gone public with allegations of him beating her and, in August 1988, Tyson breaks a bone in his hand after an infamous 4am altercation with former opponent Mitch Green in Harlem - further pushing back any proposed fight with Frank Bruno. Tyson then crashed his BMW into a tree and reports swirl that it was a suicide attempt. By late 1988, Mike Tyson is making more headlines for his personal troubles than as a boxer. Before the fight with Spinks, Tyson told the media he was happiest in the ring because he could escape from his troubles. Now he didn't even seem to want to fight.

The world of Mike Tyson had one of its most bizarre interludes next when he was interviewed with wife Robin Givens by Barbara Walters on ABC. Mike barely says a word but Robin says plenty - few of them nice about Mike. She tells Walters that Tyson is frightening. Tyson later says Robin Givens and her scheming mother wanted to provoke a reaction from him on air. When they went home after the interview, Tyson went berserk and threatened Givens. Robin Givens filed for divorce that same month.

Tyson has to pay Robin Givens $10 million for the divorce. Givens also sued Tyson for $125 million for defamation. Despite the reported windfall Givens had allegedly landed, Robin Givens later said she never got a penny of any of this money from Tyson. Other reports though allege that Givens and her mother took $6 million out of Tyson's bank account and one of his houses. Robin Givens denied she was a gold digger who only married Tyson for his money - even putting out a statement to say as much.

Robin Givens said that her marriage to Tyson crumbled after

she suffered a miscarriage. Tyson claimed though that Robin was never pregnant to begin with and didn't put on an ounce of weight. After her split with Tyson, Robin Givens dropped out of the limelight and worked steadily as an actor. She never became a big star but she was in a Spike Lee film and shows like The Fresh Prince of Bel-Air. In the end Givens was in a lot of television movies and even a soap opera.

Robin Givens eventually had two children and remarried. She released a memoir in 2007 called Grace Will Lead Me Home which, all things considered, was reasonably kind to Mike Tyson. Robin had missed the boat though when it came to her book. If it had been released in the late 1980s or early 1990s it would have been a bestseller. By 2007 though there were few people who even remembered who Robin Givens was.

Tyson now signed an agreement with Don King. King had got his man at last. Cus D'Amato was doubtless spinning in his grave. "The leeches are out now," says Tyson's trainer Kevin Rooney. He's soon fired for his troubles. Kevin Rooney sued Mike Tyson for $49 million for breach of contract after being fired. Rooney was eventually awarded $4 million - most of which went to lawyers and the taxman. Rooney ended up training Vinny Pazienza, which was nice, but chump change compared to being Tyson's trainer.

Most boxing experts believe that Tyson declined after leaving Rooney. Tyson no longer had the same discipline and no longer trained as hard. Tyson even seemed to forget the 'peek-a-boo' defensive style drilled into him by Rooney and D'Amato. After leaving the Mike Tyson circus, Kevin Rooney went back to running Cus D'Amato's old gym in the Catskills. Though he was open to a reconciliation, Rooney said that Tyson never called him anymore.

Mike Tyson would later express some regret at how he parted ways with Kevin Rooney. Tyson said that had he been older and more mature he might have figured a way to keep Kevin onboard. Tyson is not even 23 and he's now managed to estrange himself from all the people who made him a famous boxer. The reason why Kevin Rooney left Tyson is that he hated Don King and knew Don king would end up screwing Tyson financially. The thought of being in camp with a load of Don King flunkies was more than Rooney could stand.

Don King was known in boxing as 'Teflon Don' for good reason. He's cheated boxers out of millions, been investigated numerous times for tax evasion and insurance fraud, and used his influence with boxing organisations to rig ratings and get his boxers title fights. Nothing ever quite stuck on his slippery customer though. A lawyer who cross-examined King in court during one of his many tax evasion cases said King was the most intelligent and tricky person he had ever questioned. Don King read voraciously was he was in prison as a younger man and emerged with that booming windy loquacious Shakespeare quoting manner that so charmed journalists and boxers who didn't know any better.

Mike Tyson ended 1988 by being sued by a woman claiming he'd grabbed her behind in a nightclub.

In 1988, a baby was born to Amber and John Fury in Manchester, England. After mulling over names they decided to name the baby after Mike Tyson. And so the baby's name became Tyson Fury.

Tyson's fight with Frank Bruno had been called off several times but was now switched to the United States and arranged for Las Vegas in February, 1989. Bruno probably didn't deserve the fight but he was marketable because he was British and had a big following in his home country.

The Tyson/Bruno fight was supposed to be at Wembley Stadium in London. The fight would have sold out Wembley but was now going to take place in a smaller indoor venue. The change of venue meant Tyson was going to earn about $3 million less in Las Vegas than he would have done in London. Bill Cayton, now an outside observer, wryly noted that Don King was already costing Mike money before Tyson had even entered the ring.

The 27 year-old Bruno was a magnificently sculpted heavyweight and a big puncher but he was thought to have a stamina problem and had never seemed to learn how to hold when hurt. Although he was often wrongly dubbed "weak chinned" by American pundits it was the stamina and lack of savvy that seemed destined to stop Bruno from ever becoming a world champion. In his two defeats, Bruno had been boxing well against Bonecrusher Smith and Tim Witherspoon respectively until the end. He was well ahead of Smith on points when he was caught and just seemed to freeze as punches rained down in the last round. Against Witherspoon in a 1986 title challenge, Bruno appeared to run out of gas in the eleventh round of what had been a relatively even fight for the most part.

Bruno had been inactive for over a year to preserve his Tyson payday but it hardly seemed to matter as no one gave him a chance anyway. His last contest was an eighth round stoppage of a comebacking Joe Bugner in London at the end of 1987. It was a huge domestic fight in Britain because Bugner had irritated British fans by decamping to Australia and rebranding himself "Aussie Joe". Bugner was about as Australian as Mike Tyson but the Aussies were happy to take any boxers they could get. In truth, Bugner had always been the man in the black hat in British boxing ever since he won a highly controversial decision over the beloved Henry Cooper for the domestic title in the early seventies. Bruno was the most popular British boxer since Cooper and his battering of the faded Bugner only increased his popularity. It was hard to see though how the upright, mechanical Bruno could hope to last long against prime time Tyson.

The week of the Tyson/Bruno fight, Don King endeared himself to no one when he said that Bruno would go back to England in an 'incapacitated state'. Tyson entered the ring to fight Bruno on the 25th of February 1989, less than a fortnight after his divorce from Robin Givens. Celebrities at ringside for the Tyson/Bruno included Arnold Schwarzenegger, Sylvester Stallone, Muhammad Ali, Sugar Ray Leonard, Sting, Pierce Brosnan, Jon Bon Jovi, Luther Vandross and Whitney Houston.

No sooner had the fight begun when Bruno took a knee after Tyson quickly rushed him with a volley of punches, staggered him inside and then sort of cuffed him down with a right that seemed to graze the top of Bruno's head. It looked as if a repeat of his wipeout of Spinks was on the cards. But Bruno, in a brave if ultimately futile stand, started to fight back when he got up. He held Tyson with his long arms and clubbed him around the back of the head. He had a point deducted for holding but it proved if nothing else that the big Londoner would not be intimidated and had been taught how to grapple in the gym.

Before the first round was over, Tyson moved in close and was caught by right-hook and then a short left-hook. His legs did a funny dance for a second and he appeared to be wobbled but Bruno couldn't land any follow up punches and the chance of a monumental upset faded. This was the first time that Mike Tyson had ever been visibly wobbled by a punch in the professional boxing ring.

Tyson gradually took control of the fight thereafter, his handspeed too much for the challenger. Bruno was stopped in the fifth as Tyson punished him against the ropes with a vicious assault. Bruno had fought valiantly though and gave Tyson a much tougher fight than Spinks, Tubbs, Holmes, and most of the others had. It had been a somewhat shambling performance by Tyson and with his personal life in meltdown one could hardly blame him for being distracted.

The Bruno fight was considered by many to be Tyson's worst performance at the time. His timing was off and Bruno hit more him than anyone else had managed to do. Some felt that Bruno, with his roughhouse tactics, had actually provided a blueprint for how to beat Tyson.

There was more personal trouble for Tyson in the spring of 1989 when he was accused of hitting a parking attendant outside a nightclub in Los Angeles. The carefully protected image that Jim Jacobs had once tried to engineer for Tyson was blown to the winds by now.

Tyson only fought once more in 1989 when he took on Carl "The Truth" Williams. Carl "The Truth" Williams was a tall, talented heavyweight with a superb jab. He took Larry Holmes to a disputed points decision in a 1985 title fight but then seemed to be eliminated from the heavyweight sweepstakes when the veteran Mike Weaver stopped him in the second. But in 1987 Williams got right back into contention when he upset the streaking powerpuncher Bert Cooper with a stoppage after eight rounds.

Bert Cooper was from the Frazier stable and so carried the sobriquet "Smokin'". A short, compact puncher like Tyson,

Cooper was hot stuff for a while and after he demolished the Canadian hope Willie de Wit thoughts had turned to a Cooper v Tyson fight. Williams boxed superbly and took Cooper's place in the Tyson lottery, exposing Bert's limitations against big heavyweights. If Williams - with his height and great jab - could defuse an explosive slugger like Cooper than perhaps he might be in with a chance of doing the same to Tyson? The most salient objection to this line of speculation was that Williams was not known for his sturdy chin. And Mike Tyson was not Bert Cooper.

Tyson seemed better able to put external distractions to one side against Carl Williams than he had done against Bruno in January. A perfect left-hook collapsed the huge challenger early on and although he rose to his feet and told the referee he was ok the contest was terminated at 1:33 of the first round. Williams and his corner protested vehemently at the stoppage but it was hard to see the point of him carrying on. Tyson would have nailed him again sooner or later. The stoppage was definitely premature though. You can be quite sure that the referee wouldn't have stopped the fight if it had been Tyson who hit the canvas early.

Mike Tyson earned $4 million for the Williams fight. It wasn't that long ago that Bill Cayton had got him $21 million for the Spinks fight. After the Williams fight, Don King made great play of giving Tyson $100,000 in cash because Tyson had bet him he'd win in the first round. $100,000 was loose change to Don King. The fight with Carl Williams was the last time anyone would see Tyson in the ring in 1989.

Tyson returned to the ring in February 1990, back at the Tokyo Dome to fight James 'Buster' Douglas. The fight with Buster Douglas was presumed a mere warm-up for Tyson's next superfight. The brilliant former cruiserweight champion

Evander Holyfield was now campaigning as a heavyweight and had established himself as the number one contender. Pundits doubted that Holyfield had the power to keep Tyson at bay but he was clearly the most credible challenge out there while a gaggle of prospects led by Riddick Bowe, Lennox Lewis and Ray Mercer were still learning their trade.

Buster was a notoriously up and down boxer who once suffered the indignity of being stopped by journeyman Mike "the Giant" White. He seemed to have a conditioning problem and it was this lack of stamina that enabled Tony Tucker to come from behind and force a late stoppage when he fought Douglas for the vacant IBF title a few years ago. Douglas had rebounded with several wins over some decent names like Oliver McCall and Trevor Berbick but no one thought he had a prayer against Tyson. Some oddsmakers were offering 42-1 for anyone willing to bet on Buster Douglas beating Tyson.

By now Tyson was being trained by Aaron Snowell and Jay Bright. Bright was a friend from the D'Amato days in Catskill. He was actually an actor and not a boxer or trainer. It was a standing joke that Bright's main contribution to the house of Cus was his ability to make a good quiche. "Cus would be spinning in his grave if he knew Jay Bright was training Tyson," sighed Teddy Atlas. Hardly anyone in boxing knew who Aaron Snowell, Tyson's other new trainer, was at the time. His main claim to fame was being in Tim Witherspoon's corner when Witherspoon gave Larry Holmes a torrid fight.

Kevin Rooney continued to give interviews at this time saying that Tyson should get back with him. Rooney seemed to cling to an unrealistic hope that Tyson would come to his senses and drive back to that little Catskill gym. It could be the case that it finally dawned on Rooney how much money he had missed out on by becoming estranged from Tyson. Rooney had no regrets though. There was never any doubt that he would side with Bill Cayton against Don King. It may have cost Rooney his job and tens of millions of dollars but there was more to life than money.

There were some portents in the run up to the Tyson/Douglas fight that hindsight (always a wonderful gift) alert us to but no one at the time thought that the contest would be anything other than another routine Tyson knockout victory. Some footage emerged of Tyson being decked while sparring with former WBA champion Greg Page but the incident was largely chalked off as a conspiracy designed at selling some more tickets. Don King was thinking about a Tyson v Page fight in the near future and who wouldn't put it past him to stage a bit of mischief like this?

Meanwhile, Buster Douglas was motivated by the death of his mother only 23 days before the contest. He promised to win the fight for her. The mother of Buster's child also fell ill with a kidney complaint. Buster promised to win the fight for her too. Mike Tyson would later say that on the eve of the Douglas fight he slept with two women. Tyson simply didn't want to train like he used to. The old dedication was gone.

The Tyson/Douglas fight was a surreal event, the huge Tokyo superdome deathly quiet. The polite Japanese crowd barely made a sound as the unbelievable unfolded in the ring.

Buster uses his height and handspeed to box Tyson's ears off in the opening rounds. We have seen Tyrell Biggs and Tony Tubbs start well against Tyson and then fall apart once he closes the distance and begins to unload but this time it's different. A glum looking Tyson seems disinterested and the upper body movement and combinations that made him so spectacular are noticeable by their absence. He's looking for the one big bomb but that strategy is useless against Douglas in the early rounds.

Buster looks like a man reborn, snapping jabs and right-hands out, beating Tyson to the punch. It's the first time we've seen Tyson take a beating in the ring and he suddenly seems shrunken and strangely plausible. Douglas looks huge in comparison. What is noticeable in the Douglas fight is how Tyson doesn't move his head the way he used to when he was trained by Kevin Rooney. This makes him much easier to hit. Douglas also beats Tyson to the punch - which is amazing given that Tyson's handspeed is a trademark and Buster is supposed to be lazy and lethargic.

The Don King cronies running Tyson's corner in the Buster Douglas fight forgot the End-Swell (a device to treat facial bruising during a fight) and are reduced to filling a latex glove with water to use instead. The thought that Tyson might get hit during the fight never occurred to them. They were clearly expecting another early kayo win.

In the eighth round a battered Tyson seems as if he's managed to clutch victory from the jaws of defeat when he nails a complacent Douglas with a huge uppercut. But Douglas is up at the count of nine (it's obvious he was composed enough to listen to the count and give himself as much time as possible to recover) and although Tyson tries to launch a desperation attack in the ninth, Buster is soon back in charge.

In the tenth a brutal barrage by Douglas sends Tyson crashing to the canvas. The groggy soon to be ex-champion has no control of his faculties and in his woozy state tries to pick up his gumshield and shove it back in his mouth. He staggers unsteadily to his feet as the referee wraps protective arms around him and signals that the fight is over. It is perhaps the most shocking upset in sporting history.

Don King's disgraceful and shameless attempt to reverse the decision of this fight is incredible. He claims that Buster recieved a "long count" in the eighth and that the fight should be declared a kayo victory for Tyson. King manages to get WBC boss Jose Sulaiman (Sulaiman and King were thick as thieves) onboard briefly but - overnight - even this dubious duo realise that what they are thinking about doing is just plain wrong and that they will be castigated by the press.

Don King's fury comes down to a simple equation. With Tyson no longer in possession of the belts, King no longer controls the heavyweight division. It used to be said that whoever controlled Prague controlled Europe. The heavyweight division was King's metaphorical Prague. When Buster Douglas announced plans to make his first defence against the Duva family controlled Evander Holyfield all of King's nightmares coalesced. Don King was suddenly on the outside looking in.

Mike Tyson later said that by the Buster Douglas fight he no longer enjoyed boxing. Once it had been his passion but now it was simply a job. To round off Tyson's miserable 1990, he was sued by Phyllis Polaner, former aide to Robin Givens, for sexual assault and harassment. A New York City civil jury also finds Tyson committed battery against Sandra Miller.

# CHAPTER THREE (1990 - 1997)

As Buster Douglas made arrangements to fight Holyfield and Tyson and King contemplated their next move, a curious sideshow was gaining prominence with the comeback of former heavyweight champion George Foreman. After he lost to Jimmy Young in 1977 Foreman had what he believed to be a mystical experience (his trainer Gil Clancy simply put it down to heat prostration). He left boxing and became a Baptist minister but a decade later Foreman found that his attempts to fund a Youth Center in his native Houston were rapidly eating into his savings and decided to make a boxing comeback.

Foreman been out of the ring for ten years when he returned in 1987 and was 38 years old (although whispers in boxing said George was older than he claimed). He was not far off 300 pounds and swapped his diet of hamburgers and pizzas for chicken and fish to shed weight. Foreman soon became something of a cult figure with his ancient trainer Archie Moore and habit of standing between rounds with his foot on the stool surveying the crowd. His comeback was treated as a sad circus act by the boxing press at first. However, Foreman eventually confounded the sceptics. In 1994, at the age of 45, at a time when Mike Tyson was languishing in prison, Foreman stopped the young undefeated Michael Moorer in the 10th round to become the WBA world heavyweight champion. Quite a feat.

Foreman had reinvented himself during his comeback, the surly sullen character of the seventies replaced by the genial wisecracking "Big George". He fought in a lot of 'tank towns' and was criticised for the careful selection of his opponents but - unbelievably - Foreman was becoming a hugely marketable option for Tyson and the winner of Douglas/Holyfield. Thoughts turned to his destruction of the Tyson-esque Joe Frazier back in the day. What if he nailed an oncoming Tyson wih one of those uppercuts? George seemed to have retained the bonejarring power of his youth (as the axiom goes, the last thing a boxer loses is his punch)

A Tyson v Foreman fight may have once seemed like a bizarre proposition only viewable for time travellers but it didn't seem so crazy a notion by 1990. Tyson needed to get back in the ring sooner rather than later and he was placed on a June double-header in Las Vegas with Big George. Tyson would meet his old amateur rival Henry Tillman while Foreman would meet the Brazilian fringe contender Adilson Rodrigues. If they both won then a Tyson v Foreman fight was a strong possibility.

After the Buster Douglas fiasco, Don King decided Tyson needed a new trainer. The man he hired was someone he'd known since the old days in Cleveland - Richie Giachetti. Richie Giachetti had worked for Don King for years - most famously with Larry Holmes when Holmes was champion. He was a straight talking Italian-American of pudgy appearance. Giachetti sported a facial scar which he picked up in a bar fight years ago. Giachetti was a good motivator and a tough character.

Richie Giachetti actually taught Sly Stallone to box for the film Rocky. Giachetti was also a technical advisor on Rocky IV and coached Dolph Lundgren to play Ivan Drago. Richie Giachetti's appointment as Tyson's trainer did not impress Bill Cayton and Kevin Rooney because Giachetti had been critical of Cus D'Amato and Cus had disliked him. Cayton went as far to say that hiring Giachetti was a deliberate insult by King. This seemed a bit over the top. Jay Bright, the only link to Cus left in Tyson's camp, stayed on and worked under Richie Giachetti. At this time, Don King also hired veteran cutman Eddie Aliano to be in the corner. They didn't want a repeat of what happened in the Douglas fight where Tyson's corner were all at sea.

The two people running Tyson's camp now were John Horne

and Rory Holloway - who were old friends of Tyson. They were his managers and camp co-ordinators. It was certainly a far cry from the days of Jacobs and Cayton. Horne is the man who later complained about Holyfield 'jumping around like a little bitch' after Tyson bit part of his ear off.

Despite his success as an amateur (heavyweight gold at the Los Angeles Olympics), Tyson's opponent Henry Tillman, a blown-up cruiserweight, had proved fragile at the top echelons of the professional ranks and was chosen so that Tyson could get a morale boosting quick kayo after the Douglas shocker. Henry had seen better days and was regarded to be "chinny" by those in the trade. He had four losses and both Evander Holyfield and the unheralded Dwain Bonds had stopped him.

A jittery looking Tillman was rescued at 2:47 the first round against Tyson and no one was too surprised. With so little evidence to digest it was hard to know against Tillman if Tyson had lost anything or if the Buster loss was a blip caused by overconfidence and a lack of preparation. Meanwhile, Foreman kept up his side of the bargain by effortlessly dispatching Rodrigues inside two rounds on the Tyson/Tillman undercard.

Tyson had looked more defined and faster against Tillman but his timing was a bit off - which was probably to be expected. There were essentially three Mike Tyson eras in boxing - the young unbeaten Tyson (1985-1989), the post-Buster Douglas Tyson (1990-1991), and the post-prison Tyson (1995-2005). It was fairly easy to rank these. Tyson's prime was 1988. The early 90s Tyson was still formidable but not the same fighter. The post-prison Tyson could still punch hard and still had some of that intimidation factor but, ultimately, was a lot more beatable than in the two previous eras of Tyson.

It was noticeable after the Tillman win that Tyson was interviewed by Jim Lampley on HBO rather than Larry Merchant. Don king didn't like Merchant because he thought Larry was too critical of Tyson.

That October, the boxing world tuned away from the comebacking Tyson to focus on the Douglas v Holyfield fight. It was a fascinating match-up on paper. Could Buster fight with the same motivation he'd displayed against Tyson? Was Holyfield big enough to compete at heavyweight? Could he negate Buster's size advantage? The fearless predictors were split but the actual fight proved to be a dreadful anti-climax.

Buster was hopelessly overweight and fought like a man thinking about what he might have for dinner that evening rather than a man defending the world heavyweight championship. When Douglas went down in the third he appeared to be perfectly capable of getting up but seemed to make a conscious decision to stay on the canvas. Buster Douglas was soon forgotten and when Holyfield's camp decided that they wanted to fight Foreman next (their reasoning was that it was a huge payday with relatively little risk given Foreman's age) Tyson was out in the cold.

Tyson was in a strange sort of limbo at this time because despite being the most famous and marketable boxer in the world he was shut out of the heavyweight picture. Imagine how Don King felt to have heavyweight title fights take place without him. All that money going to some other promoter! During this period Tyson would get embarrassed when someone announced him as the heavyweight champion at a club or function. Tyson would remind them he was merely the ex-champion. He desperately wanted his old titles back.

Tyson was still in good shape now but he wasn't the training fiend of his early days. He smoked and took drugs in private. He also liked to drink beer. Tyson's diet as a fighter was oatmeal for breakfast, chicken for lunch, and steak and pasta for dinner. On a cheat day he liked to indulge in ice cream. Tyson would much later become a vegan although he went back to eating a little bit of meat in the end.

Tyson was supposed to be back in the ring in September 1990 but a cut in sparring meant it was December before he fought again. His opponent was Alex "The Destroyer" Stewart.

Stewart was born in in London and fought for Jamaica as an amateur before settling in New York. He'd won all of his fights by knockout and in his only loss fought bravely against Evander Holyfield before being stopped in the eighth round. Holyfield aside, Stewart had fought no one of note and so his impressive sounding 26-1 record was regarded to be flattering to say the least.

Stewart had ample motivation because his manager Mike Jones had sadly died of a sudden illness recently. Come fight night though, Stewart succumbed to the Tyson intimidation factor. He looked petrified and went down from practically the first punch Tyson launched in his direction. Poor Alex never really got himself together and with the three knockdown rule in effect the fight was predictably over before the first round had ended.

By now, Don King, irritated by Larry Merchant's perfectly valid discussion and even criticism of Tyson on HBO, moved Tyson from HBO to Showtime. Tyson's title fights had all been on HBO so it was the end of an era. HBO got the prime of Tyson. Showtime got the Tyson who was on the way down - albeit slowly at first. Somehow it wasn't quite the same having Tyson on Showtime. Showtime had plenty of money but nothing could ever quite match the sense of occasion and style that HBO lent to their boxing broadcasts with Jim Lampley and Larry Merchant.

With Holyfield v Foreman booked for April, Don King looked for an alternative opponent who was credible and liable to make people who were tired of first round knockouts willing to stump up some pay-per view money. Enter Donovan "Razor" Ruddock, a Canadian heavyweight who, after a slow start as a professional, was becoming a hot property with some fearsome knockouts.

Ruddock's brutal fourth round knockout over Michael Dokes was reminiscent of Gerry Cooney's one round blowout of Ken Norton and while Dokes, like Norton, had seen better days no one disputed that Tyson v Razor was an attractive and potentially explosive encounter. Ruddock was not intimidated by Tyson and his hybrid left-hook/uppercut (known as The Smash) would give even Iron Mike something to be wary of.

Tyson battled demons outside the ring who couldn't be kayoed with a left-hook. Drugs and alcohol. Tyson would become a full blown cocaine addict and his lifestyle (you can take the boy out of the ghetto but you cannot take the ghetto out of the boy) became increasingly unconducive to remaining at the top of the boxing world. Long since diagnosed with depressive problems, Tyson's behaviour would become increasingly erratic with some of his verbal insults at Ruddock bordering on the bizarre.

Although he had displayed some of the old power and killer instinct since his loss to Douglas, Tyson would never manage to get it completely back together while he was still young enough to do so. Only in fleeting snatched fragments. Tyson was a high energy fighter who was effective because he had fast hands, punched in combination, and could keep the pressure on for every minute of every round. There is an obvious problem with that style. It is a young man's style. Once the speed and reflexes began to erode and bad training habits crept in, Tyson was no longer the same.

Tyson and Ruddock met at the Mirage Hotel & Casino in March, 1991. It was a bruising encounter with Ruddock hitting the canvas in the second and third rounds. He refused to fold though and gamely hung in there, even seeming to hurt Tyson in the sixth round when he managed to get off some of his own bombs.

In the seventh Tyson took control and staggered Ruddock, the big Canadian reeling back against the ropes. At this point referee Richard Steele - a controversial figure already because of his disputed though humane action in waving off the Julio César Chávez v Meldrick Taylor fight with seconds to go in 1990 - stopped the contest despite Ruddock appearing to be capable of carrying on. A riot broke out in the ring after the Tyson/Ruddock ending with both camps joining in the melee. There was only thing to do and that was get them back in the ring. Don King prepared the sequel for June.

Meanwhile, in April 1991, Holyfield made the first defence of his world championship against Foreman. Holyfield was 28 and Foreman was 42. Was Big George a phenom or a fraud who had conned his way to a payday? The last thing boxing needed was a black eye again and Holyfield hammering George to an early defeat would have been that black eye. But George lasted the full twelve rounds in a performance (albeit a losing one) that had previously sceptical pundits admitting that Foreman was pretty amazing. He'd restored his honour and that of boxing. The deck was clear for Tyson v Holyfield or at least the negotiations, but first Tyson had to deal with

Ruddock again.

The fracas that ended the first fight had involved Ruddock's promoter Murad Muhammad and Tyson's trainer Richie Giachetti becoming involved in handbags at zero paces. Muhammad was suspended by Nevada Athletic Commission and Ruddock threatened to pull out of the fight but all was resolved in the end.

King and Tyson had their own worries too when Holyfield's camp seemed to suggest that his next fight would be a rematch with Foreman. They appeared to be trying to lock Tyson out of the title picture. Holyfield was promoted by the New Jersey based Main Events of Duva family fame. The Duva family were not known for their love of Don King. Razor Ruddock was apparently willing to step aside (for a fee) to make way for a Tyson v Holyfield fight but in the end he didn't have too. The boxing press at the time simply wanted Tyson v Holyfield for the title. They didn't really want Tyson v Ruddock II or Holyfield v Foreman II.

Tyson's frame of mind in the preamble to the second Ruddock fight was increasingly strange and confrontational. A palpable aura of self-destruction and turmoil. Tyson demolished the $20,000 lens of an ABC television camera, snarling "Get outta my face you f**k!" and in a television interview to promote the fight he told a bemused looking Ruddock that he wanted to "kiss those big lips of yours and make you my girlfriend."

The Tyson/Ruddock rematch was a brutal one full of low-blows, hitting after the bell and brawling violence. Ruddock hit the canvas twice and was hurt several times while Tyson had points deducted for various infractions. Ruddock ended the evening with a broken jaw and a closed eye and lost the fight on points by a wide distance. Tyson had won but the bruising encounter indicated once again that he wasn't quite the fighter that he used to be.

The next step for Tyson was obvious. Get Evander Holyfield in the ring and win the title back. The impasse was broken and the fight was announced for November 1991. Bob Arum (who was Foreman's promoter) was furious as he thought that George Foreman was supposed to fight Holyfield again. He'd been trumped by his arch nemesis King on this occasion. But the best laid plans of King were about to be scuppered by events that would put Tyson out of boxing for four years.

In July, 1991, Mike Tyson was a guest judge at the Miss Black America pageant in Indianapolis, Indiana. There is some footage of a leering Tyson being introduced to Desiree Washington and other young women at the event. Eighteen year-old Desiree Washington, who had been crowned Miss Black Rhode Island, was an incoming college freshman. Desiree was invited to come out later by Tyson. It was apparently because her father was a big Mike Tyson and boxing fan that Desiree accepted. She thought it would be great if she could get Tyson's autograph for her dad.

Tyson invited Desiree to his hotel room to talk. She made it clear to him that she was not interested in a one-night stand but alleged that Tyson then raped her. The next day Desiree Washington checked into the emergency room at Methodist Hospital and said she'd been raped. Three days after the incident, Desiree Washington went to the police to report Mike Tyson.

Mike Tyson was arrested and his career now hung in the balance. A special grand jury indicts Tyson on rape and three other charges. Two days later, he is booked in Indianapolis and released on a $30,000 cash bond. Don King hired Vincent

Fuller to defend Tyson at the trial. Fuller, whose services cost King $5,000 a day, had got King off a tax-evasion charge in the past and so Don had a high regard for his ability. He presumed that Fuller would swiftly get Tyson out of this trouble and secure an innocent verdict.

The jury for the trial was mostly male and mostly white. Tyson's team were not happy about this at all. Strange as it may seem now in an age of #MeToo, public sympathy was largely with Tyson. He also had the black community broadly on his side. With the exception of Michael Jackson, Tyson was the most famous celebrity in America. Tyson was a hero to many. A lot of people seemed to assume, or at least hope, that Desiree Washington was some sort of fantasist or gold digger and that these charges were bogus.

To the dismay of Don King, it soon transpired in court that Vincent Fuller, the expensive attorney he'd hired to defend Tyson, wasn't doing a very good job. Fuller's area expertise was tax fraud and white collar crime cases. He had no experience of sex crime cases. Fuller also seemed to know little about Indiana law.

The trial did not start well for Tyson. Tyson's limousine driver Virginia Foster, who had been hired to ferry him around Indianapolis, gave evidence and told the court that Desiree Washington got into the limo after the alleged rape and seemed dazed, distressed, and upset. Virginia Foster also told the court that Tyson had tried to fondle her after he lured Foster into his hotel room.

A doctor at the hospital where Desiree Washington was treated told the court that he had only seen injures like the ones on Desiree a few times and in both of those cases a rape had taken place. The strategy of Tyson's defence team in the trial was obvious. They would have to prove that Tyson's encounter with Desiree Washington was consensual and that she knew full well what she was doing and what she was getting into when she went into his hotel room.

In order to prove that the encounter was consensual and Desiree Washington was not as innocent as she was making out, Vincent Fuller questioned numerous witnesses from the Miss Black America pageant who all testified that Tyson was crude and flirtatious. Fuller's aim was to show the court that Desiree Washington must have seen this for herself. She must have been aware of Mike Tyson's reputation. She must have known why he wanted to go to her room. Fuller argued that Desiree Washington consented to her encounter with Tyson and had many chances to avoid it - none of which she took. There was a very obvious flaw in the strategy of Fuller in court. It basically painted Mike Tyson as a creepy and dangerous sex pest.

Mike Tyson seemed in a faraway trance during the trial. He doodled on a piece of paper and looked bored. Tyson didn't look like someone with much expectation of getting away with this.

Desiree Washington was detailed when she took the stand. She said that she had got her purse to leave but Tyson had pinned her down and raped her. Vincent Fuller gave
Desiree Washington a fairly easy ride in his questioning - which was obviously not what he was supposed to be doing. He failed to pin Desiree Washington down on any possible inconsistencies.

The trial got even worse for the defence when Mike Tyson gave evidence. He was destroyed by the prosecution. Tyson came across as crude and unemotional. His statements also clashed with the evidence given by the limousine driver Virginia Foster. In February 1992, Mike Tyson is convicted of rape and sentenced to 10 years in prison - four suspended.

Tyson's behaviour had caught up with him at last. His womanising, fast living, his dangerous sense of entitlement. To borrow an obvious line that did the rounds - Iron Mike had become Leg-Iron Mike. The world of boxing would spin on without him for the foreseeable future.

Desiree Washington was a distinguished student who couldn't be paid off or tarnished. After the trial she said that a one million dollar 'bribe' had been offered to her to drop the case but she had refused to accept this. Desiree Washington gave a television interview after the trial for Barbara Walters on ABC. Washington said that Tyson should stay in prison until he is rehabilitated. She said that she was doing him a service because he might now consider his conduct and become a better person. After the Barbara Walters interview, Desiree Washington dropped out of sight and was never heard from again.

As you might imagine, this was all Don King's worst nightmare. His cash cow in prison. Mega money fights with Holyfield and Foreman now impossible. A desperate Don King now hired Alan Dershowitz to represent Tyson. Alan Dershowitz is a lawyer who has represented many big celebrities in his career. He was part of the team that, somehow, got OJ Simpson off his murder charge.

Alan Dershowitz sought to overturn Mike Tyson's rape verdict by destroying the image of Desiree Washington. Dershowitz claimed he had evidence that Washington had once falsely accused another young man of rape. Dershowitz also claimed he had new evidence that Desiree Washington had been seen kissing and groping Tyson before they went to his hotel room. The appeal by Alan Dershowitz was ultimately unsuccessful. Mike Tyson would remain in prison and serve his time.

Tyson would later claim that going to prison was the best thing that ever happened to him. It may have even saved his life. Tyson adjusted to life inside prison, ducking and diving, having illicit encounters with women, taking a break from the drugs that were damaging him on the outside. Tyson had celebrity visitors, access to the telephone and started to train and lose weight with view to recapturing the championship. It wasn't paradise but he could see how people became institutionalised if they got stuck in these places for too long.

While in prison, Tyson had tattoos of the tennis player Arthur Ashe, Chinese communist leader Mao Zedong, and Marxist revolutionary Che Guevara. Tyson failed his high school diploma examination while in prison. If he'd passed he would have got a shorter sentence.

While he was in prison Tyson also became a Muslim. As his release date neared it led to talk about who would control his career if - as assumed - he tried to make a boxing comeback. There was speculation that Tyson, in light of his conversation to the Muslim faith, might sign with Murad Muhammad. Murad Muhammad was an African-American promoter who worked with boxers like James Scott, Matthew Saad Muhammad, and Eddie Mustafa Muhammad. However, when the 28 year-old Tyson was released on March the 25th, 1995, after serving 3½ years of a 10-year sentence, he re-signed with Don King.

While Tyson had been away in prison the heavyweight division had fragmented into a confused mess. The lightly regarded Bruce Seldon was the WBA champion after a win over the shopworn Tony Tucker while Oliver McCall - Tyson's former sparring partner - had upset Lennox Lewis to win the WBC title in 1994. McCall defended the title with a points win over the ancient Larry Holmes and then lost on a decision to Frank Bruno in London. It was Bruno's fourth attempt to win a world title and McCall's unmotivated performance saw Bruno home.

After losing and then regaining his title against Riddick Bowe, Evander Holyfield had put in a strangely lethargic and passive performance in a points loss to Michael Moorer. Moorer's trainer was Teddy Atlas - who had once been Tyson's amateur trainer until banished from D'Amato's camp for taking a stand against Tyson's conduct when it came to girls. Atlas had now coached his own fighter to the heavyweight championship. Evander Holyfield was said to have a heart defect and people wondered if he'd ever fight again. They needn't have wondered because Holyfield proved to be incapable of retiring and would fight on.

Meanwhile, just to complete the circuitous merry-go-round, Moorer had lost his belts when he was stopped by George Foreman in the tenth round of their 1994 contest. Big George had declined to fight Tony Tucker in his first defence and so created the vacant Seldon v Tucker fight for the WBA title. Foreman kept the IBF belt and chose a German named Axel Schulz to defend against. What was supposed to be an easy defence turned out to be nothing of the kind. Schulz fought his heart out and appeared to have outpointed Foreman until Big George got a gift on the judges scorecards. Whereupon George was stripped of the IBF belt for refusing to grant Schulz a rematch. Not for the first time, George then started banging the drum for him and Tyson to meet.

The two heavyweights rated the most highly and the ones

expected to give a comebacking Tyson the most potential problems were Riddick Bowe and Lennox Lewis. Bowe was from Brownsville like Tyson and a huge 6'5 heavyweight with a good amateur pedigree. Despite his undoubted talent and raw power, Bowe sometimes seemed desperately unmotivated and was prone to putting on a lot of weight between fights. After winning the title against Holyfield he made a couple of shamefully safe and predictably one-sided defences against shot veterans Jesse Ferguson and Michael Dokes and then lost the Holyfield rematch.

The main problem for Bowe and his shrewd manager Rock Newman was that they seemed absolutely terrified of Lennox Lewis despite a Bowe v Lewis fight appearing to be a natural. Lewis had stopped Bowe in the Olympics and was the one heavyweight who could match Bowe's size and power. When he won the belts from Holyfield, Bowe dumped the WBC portion in a trash can rather than meet number one contender Lewis. So Bowe was now in a strange sort of limbo, making do with contests against the likes of Larry Donald, Herbie Hide (from whom he extracted the lightly regarded WBO bauble) and Jorge Luis González while he headed towards an inevitable third fight with the now beltless Holyfield and waited to see what would happen with Tyson's comeback.

Tyson and Bowe rarely talked about fighting each other and it seems that no serious attempt to make the fight was undertaken. The timing just never aligned for Bowe v tyson. Tyson was in prison when Bowe was in his prime and Bowe's career was fading when Tyson got out of prison. Tyson has suggested that he never wanted to fight Bowe because he saw Bowe as a kindred spirit from Brownsville.

Lennox Lewis meanwhile, after the shocking upset loss to

McCall, was well and truly locked out and having to start all over again. On Halloween night in 1992, Lewis had blitzed Tyson's old nemesis Razor Ruddock and shown his vast potential but now he had to convince everyone again. It took a while for Lewis to punch his way back to the VIP section of the division.

Tyson's comeback fight was hugely anticipated but who would be his opponent? In the end Don King chose a white pug named Peter McNeeley who he had under contract. McNeeley was a clubfighter with an inflated 36-1 record compiled against hopeless opposition. With various machinations, King ensured that Tyson would get a world ranking if he beat McNeeley and the chances of Tyson, even a rusty Tyson, losing to McNeeley were zero.

The McNeeley fight took place in August 1995 at the MGM Grand and despite the outcome being a foregone conclusion it generated a then-record $63 million in Pay-per-view buys. No one in boxing could attract attention like Tyson. Like a B-film actor suddenly given a part in a Hollywood blockbuster, McNeeley made the most of his supporting role. Even Tyson seemed to be amused when Peter promised to wrap Iron Mike in a "cocoon of horror."

The fight itself lasted ninety seconds. McNeeley charged at Tyson, flailing away with ineffective punches. Seven seconds into the fight he went down from practically the first punch Tyson threw. McNeeley was up again and re-entered the fray, flailing away at Tyson again.

Tyson - understandably - seemed a little rusty and content to let Peter expend some energy while he lined him up. When an uppercut floored McNeeley his manager Vinnie Vecchione entered the ring to stop the fight and so Tyson was awarded a disqualification victory.

Only sadists could regret the fact that Tyson hadn't been allowed to wallop the dazed McNeeley again. On the undercard, Bruce Seldon, clearly being lined up as a near future opponent for Tyson, managed to retain his WBA belt when the gutsy and popular Native American slugger Joe Hipp suffered massive facial swelling and bleeding and their fight was terminated in the tenth round.

Tyson was now dating Monica Turner. Turner, a paediatrician, first met Tyson in 1990 at a party hosted by Eddie Murphy. Monica Turner had kept in contact with Tyson when he was in prison. Tyson and Monica Turner were married in 1997 and had two children. The marriage lasted seven years before Turner left Tyson because he was carrying on with other women.

Tyson was back in the ring in December and although the opponent was a step up from McNeeley it was still a carefully selected match while Tyson prepared to fight for the WBC belt. Buster Mathis Jr was the son of the sixties heavyweight contender and although he was a decent boxer he had little power. Aside from a shopworn Tyrell Biggs, the most famous person he'd met in the ring was Riddick Bowe. Bowe knocked out Mathis when he took a knee in the fourth round and the bout was declared void (although technically Bowe should probably have been disqualified).

Tyson and Mathis met at Philadelphia's CoreStates Spectrum on the 16th of December and Tyson's ring rust was much in evidence. Mathis bobbed and weaved and clinched and Tyson seemed to miss with an awful lot of punches. Tyson managed to salvage his reputation with two right-uppercuts in the third that put Buster down for the count but the performance as a whole was not likely to strike too much fear into the hearts of Foreman, Bowe and Lewis. His next performance was a different matter entirely.

The MGM Grand is chosen as the venue for Tyson's WBC title tilt against Frank Bruno - the man he beat in five rounds in defence of his undisputed titles back in 1989. In an ideal world Bruno might possibly have liked to retire after finally winning the world title but he only got the McCall fight from Don King on condition that if he won he had to then fight Tyson again. Anyway, Tyson v Bruno II would give him an awfully big twilight payday win or lose.

Given Tyson's rusty performance against Mathis and the presumption that becoming a champion had probably done a lot for Bruno's confidence there were a lot more punters willing to risk a bet on Big Frank this time compared to 1989. Anyone who did have a flutter on the huge Englishman might have started to nurse doubts about the wisdom of gambling when he made his ring walk. Bruno did not look confident. At the very least Bruno could never be accused of not giving his all in the ring. Even in his defeats, to Smith and Witherspoon, and to Tyson in 1989 and Lennox Lewis in 1993, he had fought bravely and taken the fight to his opponent when he had the chance. Perhaps Bruno was simply never given a chance this time. Tyson was, in the words of Big Frank, "on him like a harbour shark."

On this night Tyson seemed to rekindle the flame of the eighties Tyson, the force of nature who seemed unstoppable. He was razor sharp and the combinations were back. Bruno could do little other than hold on desperately, trying his best to stave off the inevitable. A thirteen punch combination ended the fight in the third round and Tyson was the champion again. Well, he had one of the belts. It seemed like a mere formality now for him to acquire the others.

Richie Giachetti, Tyson's early 1990s trainer, was not in the corner for Tyson comeback because he'd fallen out with Don King. Giachetti had taken legal action against King for money more than once but they always seemed to patch things up in the end.

And so it was onto September the 7th, 1996 for Tyson versus the WBA champion Bruce Seldon. It was absolutely masterful 'low risk/high reward' stuff from Don King. He'd got Tyson two world title shots without having to fight anyone of note. The top heavyweights at this time were Holyfield, Lewis, Golota, Moorer, Mercer, and Bowe. Also in the top ten was the dangerous David Tua - who reminded many of the young Tyson with his short stature and big punching. Don King had studiously avoided anyone too dangerous as he eased Mike back into division's top table.

Bruce was on a winning streak that had seen him beat some decent opponents in Greg Page, Tony Tucker and Joe Hipp. Page and Tucker had seen younger days for sure but Seldon was getting better and many ranked him as the best pure boxer in the division. It counted for nothing Seldon in his fight with Tyson. Many Tyson opponents appeared beaten before the first bell but Seldon's surrender at 1:49 of the first round seemed especially abject. Seldon went down twice from punches that didn't even seem to connect cleanly.

Late in the first round, Seldon went down from a right hand which seemed to have missed the top of his left. He was then dropped by a left hook and the fight was stopped. When the replays of the knockdowns were shown in the arena the crowd started to boo and shout that the fix was in. While it was true that Seldon seem to make a meal of the punches and appeared eager to go home without taking any punishment, the idea of a fixed fight was a bit far-fetched because Mike Tyson plainly didn't need a 'fix' to beat Bruce Seldon.

The Tyson/Seldon bout was overshadowed by the shooting of rapper Tupac Shakur after the fight. He died several days later.

Meanwhile, Lennox Lewis had managed to edge himself back into the picture with wins over Tommy Morrison and Ray Mercer. Don King didn't want Tyson to fight Lewis and so had Tyson dispense with the WBC belt he'd won against Bruno. This meant that Tyson wasn't obliged to fight Lewis - who was the WBC's number one contender.

There were two reasons why King didn't want Tyson to fight Lewis. The first is that Lewis was really good and probably the best heavyweight out there. Lewis, who was 6'5 and could box and punch, would have been a very dangerous assignment for the 1997 version of Tyson. The second reason is that Lewis was promoted by Main Events. Lennox Lewis was one of those heavyweights that Don King never managed to get control of.

1996 turned out to be the year when Riddick Bowe was eliminated from the heavyweight sweepstakes. Bowe had stopped Evander Holyfield in the eighth round of their non-title rubber match in 1995 - though not before climbing off the canvas. In July, 1996, Bowe took a fearful pounding from Polish contender Andrew Golota and only won on a disqualification when Golota, despite being ahead on points, had a brainstorm and threw yet more low-blows. The exact same thing happened in the rematch - except this time Bowe took even more punishment. When he worryingly slurred his words after the fight it was obvious that Big Daddy was finished at the top echelons of the division and should retire.

Tyson, as ever, was spending money like water in real life. Buying cars and mansions that he would never even live in. He had the customary entourage of flunkies - the hangers on who get a free ride, max out the credit cards, and then vanish one day when the boxer is no longer rich or successful. One didn't need to be a financial expert to see where this was heading. If the boxing paydays ever dried up Tyson was going to be in a big hole.

Don King wanted a marketable but fairly safe fight for Tyson to end the year and came up with what he thought was the perfect answer - Evander Holyfield. The man Tyson was supposed to fight in 1991 before he went to prison. Tyson would have been a prohibitive favourite had he clashed with Holyfield in 1991 and the odds in his favour had only increased by 1996.

Since losing his titles to Michael Moorer and coming out of a brief retirement caused by a suspected heart condition (arrhythmia), Holyfield had decisioned Ray Mercer and then been stopped by Riddick Bowe in the eighth round. Holyfield's last fight before tackling Tyson was a desperately underwhelming five round victory against the former light-heavyweight champion Bobby Czyz. The 5'9 Czyz, who started his professional career as a middleweight, was having his first heavyweight bout and was dwarfed by Evander. Holyfield's sluggish performance against the overmatched Czyz had everyone fearing the worst for the Real Deal.

Tyson versus Holyfield looked like a shameful mismatch. Holyfield opened as high as a 25-1 underdog with some bookies. Budd Schulberg writes before the Tyson/Holyfield fight that this contest is purely for sadists.

The build-up to the fight found Holyfield serenely confident.

He was on a mission from God. This Bible thumping tended to irritate Tyson's camp, who argued - not unreasonably - that God probably had better things to do with his time than interfere in a prizefight. Holyfield said the difference between him and Tyson is that he had a God fearing mother who wasn't afraid to give him a clout around the ear.

One thing that was different about this fight for Tyson is that his previous post-prison opponents had all seemed terrified when they got in the ring with him and were mentally beaten before the bell rang. That wasn't the case with Holyfield. It was impossible to intimidate Holyfield. He wasn't scared of anyone.

The atmosphere was electric at the MGM Grand. People anticipated a short but explosive fight. Tyson came straight from his corner and began throwing right-hands as if he expected a brief evening's work. But Holyfield weathered the storm and soon began to fire back. Tyson took a moment to hitch his shorts up slightly and looked at Holyfield with a somewhat puzzled expression. The shot fighter he was supposed to massacre didn't seem to have turned up. "You the bully in there, he ain't the bully!" bellowed Holyfield's trainer Don Turner in the corner when the bell rang to end the first round.

Holyfield began to dig to Tyson's body and the champion quickly started to look confused, resorting to throwing single bombs which the experienced Holyfield was too savvy to fall for. The vaunted Tyson intimidation factor had no effect on Holyfield. As the second round ticked down, Holyfield span Tyson on the ropes and hammered some short hooks in. Tyson looked hurt. He was suddenly mortal again. Jay Bright appears to be Tyson's chief second but he has no idea what to say to change the course of the fight.

Holyfield is deliberately making it a messy, mauling inside fight and seems to be much stronger than Tyson. He walks Tyson around in the clinches and shoves him back, denying Iron Mike any leverage. In the fifth, Tyson managed to put together a flurry of punches at last, seeming to hurt Evander briefly with a barrage that was capped off with a stinging uppercut.

The turning of the tide doesn't last long. Tyson is cut in the sixth and Holyfield is clearly boring in with his head. Tyson looks discouraged and is dropped hard by a left-hook. It's only the second time in his career that he's been down.

The fight is the first illustration of one of the biggest weaknesses of the post-prison Tyson. Prison seemed to rob Tyson of his stamina. Tyson always had the ability to fight hard for twelve rounds - even the post-Buster Douglas version of Tyson in the early 1990s. The Holyfield fight is the first time we've seen the post-prison Tyson have to fight longer than three rounds and the first time we've seen him in a competitive contest where his opponent is actually hitting him back and providing a challenge. The post-prison Tyson is clearly not up to this challenge. His gas tank is not what it was and after a couple of rounds Tyson seemed frustrated and discouraged by Holyfield's tenacity and durability.

In the seventh Tyson is staggered by a headbutt but it is not ruled to be deliberate. Tyson is taking a pounding. The tenth round is a nightmare for Tyson. He's staggered by a right and saved by the bell when Holyfield follows up with an unanswered barrage. Tyson still looks groggy in the eleventh and is quickly staggered by left-hooks. Tyson reels away and the referee waves it over as Holyfield begins to hammer him again. Tyson is an ex-champion for the second time.

The inevitable Tyson/Holyfield rematch was set for June the 28th, 1997. Don King dubbed it The Sound and the Fury. Tyson's loss was a huge shock. in a poll of 50 boxing writers before the fight only one (Ron Borges) had picked Holyfield to win. Borges said he picked Holyfield because of an incident he witnessed between Holyfield and Tyson at an amateur training camp in 1984. "One night they were all playing pool at the Olympic Training Centre and it was one of those deals where if you lost, you gave up the table," said Borges."Tyson lost and it was Holyfield's turn to play. Tyson tried to bully him. Holyfield walked up to Tyson, didn't say a word and took the cue stick from him. Tyson left the room and nobody saw him for the rest of the night. I always had it in the back of my mind that Tyson knew if there was one guy he couldn't intimidate, it was Evander Holyfield."

Tyson married Monica Turner in New York in April and prepared for the challenge of regaining his reputation as the baddest man on the planet. Richie Giachetti was brought back by Don King to train Tyson for the rematch. Tyson hadn't really needed a trainer in his early comeback bouts but he most assuredly did need a trainer to fight Evander Holyfield again. There was no great secret about what Richie Giachetti had to do. Get Tyson using his jab, throwing combinations and presenting a more elusive target like the Tyson of the eighties used to.

Tyson's camp insisted on Mitch Halpern being replaced as referee for the rematch for allowing Holyfield to use his head too much in the first fight. The replacement was the experienced Mills Lane, a no-nonsense judge famed for his "Let's get it on!" catchphrase.

"I lost the last fight," said Tyson. "I'll correct that by winning." But Tyson was 31 now and had taken a lot of punishment in the first fight. Could he turn back the years again like he had done against Frank Bruno?

Despite the doubts suddenly swirling around his career, Tyson was the betting favourite for the Holyfield rematch and a 2-1 choice. The rematch generated a total revenue of $180 million (equivalent to $342 million adjusted for inflation). Nothing in boxing could match the allure of a Tyson fight.

The rematch took place at the same venue. The atmosphere was even more expectant. When the bell rang Holyfield seemed to carry on from where he left off last time. He looked sharper than Tyson and radiated confidence. Once again he nullified Tyson by clinching and using his superior strength.

In the second round Tyson got cut again and could clearly be seen complaining to Mills Lane about Holyfield's use of the head. Holyfield was in charge right away and Tyson looked frustrated. Tyson came out swinging in the third. He looked mad and shoved Holyfield's head back with a forearm when they wrestled inside. Tyson, as Giachetti requested, was finally using his jab and having a much better round as a consequence.

With 35 seconds of the third round to go, Tyson bit Holyfield in the ear and Holyfield turned away and began hopping around in pain. Tyson then shoved him from behind as if he was in a street fight. Everyone is now confused and isn't sure what just happened. A bewildered Mills Lane deducts two points from Tyson and the fight eventually resumes after the doctor examines Holyfield.

Now Holyfield looks mad and angry while Tyson seems to have gone crazy. They trade punches and then - astonishingly - Tyson bites Holyfield on the ear again. The extent of his second foul is only realised when the bell sounds and television replays are seen. Mills Lane can see the big screen replays of the bites too. Tyson is disqualified. The fight is over and chaos ensues as the ring fills up with people.

Tyson goes insane, trying to get at Holyfield. Tyson is even seen trying to lash out at police officers trying to restore calm. When Tyson and his entourage leave the ring the crowd jeers them and the boxer still seems pumped-up and out of control. Tyson said that after the second Holyfield fight he went home and got high.

Was it drugs, prison, alcohol, lack of training or age that caused Tyson's decline? It was all of the above and more. Tyson's life had taken its toll on the part of him that made his money as a prizefighter. Though Tyson would box on for several more years he would never become world champion again. The Holyfield rematch paved for the way for the last chapter of Tyson's boxing career. This could aptly be described as the circus freakshow years. Tyson was now a morbid curiosity.

What of Holyfield's brute strength and vastly increased muscle mass compared to his early heavyweight days? He was later implicated in investigations into athletes being supplied with illegal steroids and human growth hormone. Holyfield denies having anything to do with this (he claims he innocently took a few things he was given to treat a bout of hepatitis A) but on two separate occasions his name was thrown up when companies were raided and their client list poured over. Was Tyson fighting a "juiced" Holyffield? The use of PEDs in boxing is still a veil yet to be fully lifted.

Tyson apologised to Holyfield but was sentenced with a permanent suspension from boxing and fined $3,000,000 by the Nevada State Athletic Commission. Good riddance said many in the sport. He would have to wait a year before he could re-apply for a boxing licence.

It was the end of the Tyson gravy train for Don King. Tyson was now banned and increasingly unhappy with King. Don King, as ever, found a novel solution. He started promoting Evander Holyfield. It was King who put together the Holyfield/Lewis unification fight. King also had superstars in his stable like Felix Trinidad. He moved on from Tyson.

While Tyson contemplated life outside the ring, Lennox Lewis had regained his WBC title when Oliver McCall had a meltdown in the ring and stopped fighting. It seemed symbolic of the general madness that seemed to dog the heavyweight division at that time. Lewis, under the guidance of the great Emanuel Steward, finally began to fulfil his great potential and headed towards a megabucks unification showdown with Holyfield.

Tyson's explanation for his assault on Holyfield's tender ears is that it was retaliation for Evander's use of the head. Holyfield's tactics were rough but then the clash of heads is an occupational hazard in any boxing match. Ultimately, Tyson didn't adapt to the challenge in either fight. He didn't use his jab enough and the upper-body, head movement and rapid combinations were largely absent. Tyson just couldn't cope with Holyfield's strength, pressure, and boxing ability.

# CHAPTER FOUR (1998 - 2002)

In March, 1998, Tyson filed a $100 million lawsuit against Don King, accusing the promoter of cheating him out of $100 million. What took him so long to work out that Don King was probably not to be trusted? Hearing that Don King had allegedly skimmed off as much money as possible from his association from Tyson was like being told that it can sometimes be chilly in the North Pole.

Amongst King's many sleights of hand regarding Iron Mike's money was a $52,000 annual payment to King's daughter Debbie for being president of the Mike Tyson fan club. Nice work if you can get it! And that was merely the tip of the King iceberg. It was also claimed that Don King has used Tyson's name in lucrative commercial branding deals but never told Tyson about them or gave him any of the revenue.

Tyson was reeling from a huge tax bill and after years of ridiculous spending was now paying the price for his own stupidity and excess. "A wretched, slimy, reptilian motherf****r," said Tyson of King. "This is supposed to be my black brother right? He's just a bad man, a real bad man. He would kill his own mother for a dollar. He's ruthless, he's deplorable, he's greedy, and he doesn't know how to love anybody." Tyson later said that he attacked Don King and "stomped" him outside a hotel.

During his time away from boxing in 1998, Tyson made a guest appearance at WrestleMania XIV. Tyson was an enforcer for the main event match between Shawn Michaels and Steve Austin. Tyson was also an unofficial member of D-Generation X. He earned $3 million for his wrestling appearances.

Tyson's managers John Horne and Rory Holloway were also dismissed. Tyson had known the pair since he was a teenager. Horne and Holloway had been getting 20% of Tyson's purses. Rory Holloway, who later wrote a book about his time with

Tyson, denied accusations that he and John Horne had left Tyson's finances in a mess. Holloway said he and Horne had cut unprecedented deals for Tyson and when they left him Tyson had more money than anyone could ever need.

Tyson appointed Shelly Finkel as his new manager. Finkel, in addition to being a music promoter, had managed fighters like Meldrick Taylor, Evander Holyfield, and Pernell Whitaker in his days associated with Main Events. Shelly Finkel was a bit of a cold fish and came off as aloof and arrogant in interviews but he was highly respected in the boxing business and his fighters liked him. Years later he would manage the heavyweight Deontay Wilder and stage the Wilder/Fury trilogy. Finkel had some experience with Mike Tyson because nearly a decade previously he had been brought in as an impartial third party to get the deal over the line for Tyson to fight Michael Spinks.

When it came to Mike Tyson's $100 million lawsuit against Don King, Finkel got Mike to settle out of court for $14 million - which would be paid in installments. Kevin Rooney lambasted Finkel in the press when he heard about this. The basic accusation of Rooney is that Finkel settled the Don King lawsuit quickly (and cheaply) because he simply wanted to get Tyson back in the ring as fast as possible. Rooney felt Tyson would have won the lawsuit if Finkel had taken it all the way through the courts. Finkel - who knew a lot more business and lawsuits than Kevin Rooney - would doubtless have argued otherwise.

Tyson had now cut himself free of previous managerial and legal arrangements. He also hired Jeff Wald as an advisor. Wald had once managed the comedian Roseanne Barr and was executive producer on her sitcom.

Tyson's miserable run was complete when he was involved in a road rage incident late in 1998 and punched two drivers. It seemed short odds that Tyson would end up back in prison but he did have one piece of good news when the Nevada Athletic Commission voted 4-1 to restore his licence. Tyson had long since fallen out of love with boxing but he needed money - which was amazing really when he consider how much he had earned.

Tyson appointed a new trainer in Tommy Brooks. Brooks was highly respected and had worked with the likes of Mike McCallum, Meldrick Taylor, and Rocky Lockridge. Jay Bright was also back in Tyson's team. Bright had been dismissed after the first loss to Holyfield and wasn't in the corner for the rematch. He had patched things up with Tyson though. Bright lived in the Catskills with Camille Ewald, now in her 90s, so Mike would see him all the time when he visited Camille.

The opponent for Tyson's 1999 comeback was Frans Botha, a South African heavyweight known as The White Buffalo. Botha could box and was a tough customer but he wasn't much of a puncher and so wasn't expected to pose too many problems for Tyson. Botha had beaten Axel Schulz for the vacant IBF title in 1995 but was then stripped when he tested positive for the steroid nandrolone. Botha dubiously claimed he innocently took the drug when being treated for an arm injury. When he fought Michael Moorer for the title in his next fight he was stopped in the last round.

Tyson was paid $10 million to fight Botha. The fight with Botha was Tyson at his worst save for the ending. Botha outboxed the rust strewn Tyson with embarrassing ease and the former champion reacted by trying to break the South African's arm no less than three times, or forcibly twist it at least. The first incident of this provoked an after the bell reaction from Botha and threatened a mass brawl from either camp as the boxers were forcibly separated. Tyson was supposed to be on his best behaviour tonight but he didn't seem to have changed his ways an awful lot.

Botha continued to outbox Tyson with the greatest threat from Mike coming to the South African's arms rather than his chin. When Tyson did finally connect with a cruncher in the fifth Botha went down and failed to beat the count. The punch masked what had been a dire showing from Tyson. If he wanted another title shot he would have to sharpen up considerably.

In February, the now 32 year-old Tyson was sentenced to two years in a Maryland prison for "a dramatic example, a tragic example of potentially lethal road rage." Given that he still owed millions in taxes and $4 million to former trainer Kevin Rooney the last thing Tyson needed was to be away from his main source of income - boxing.

Even Shelly Finkel's testimony couldn't keep Tyson out of jail. It didn't help Tyson's cause that the victims were elder citizens. All it did was further cement the image of him as a bully and a thug. He was out by the end of the year and an opponent for the second comeback fight of his THIRD comeback odyssey was sought.

One name in the frame to fight Tyson next was none other than Buster Douglas. Buster had made a comeback in the mid-nineties, ostensibly for health reasons. After retiring in the wake of his dismal surrender to Holyfield, Douglas had ballooned to 400 pounds and fell into a diabetic coma. The comeback didn't amount to much though and came to an abrupt end when the white heavyweight hopeful Lou Savarese stopped him in the first round.

Buster fought a few no names as he angled for a fight against the brilliant light-heavyweight Roy Jones Jr but Tyson's brains trust decided against fighting him in the end. Buster was said to weigh 300 pounds and with Buster's punch resistance gone even a faded 32 year-old Tyson versus the 1999 version of Douglas would have been legalised manslaughter.

Tyson's team chose 34 year-old Orlin Norris as his next opponent instead. Norris was a respected boxer with a good curriculum vitae. He was the former WBA cruiserweight champion and in two campaigns at heavyweight had beaten Oliver McCall, Renaldo Snipes, Greg Page and avenged a loss against Tony Tucker (albeit a Tucker who had seen better days come the rematch).

Henry Akinwande had soundly outpointed Norris in his most recent heavyweight campaign but then the 6'8 Akinwande was a class boxer and had huge size and reach advantages over the 5'10 Norris. In his last bout before meeting Tyson, Norris had whacked out the British heavyweight prospect Pele Reid in one round. It was felt that if Tyson boxed as poorly as he did against Botha then the crafty Norris, a good fluid boxer with quick hands, would have a reasonable chance of boxing his way to a points decision.

Orlin Norris did well enough in the first round, remaining calm when Tyson tried to rush him. Orlin even started to get his jab going and used his footwork to circle away from Tyson's left hook. As the first round ended, Tyson hit Norris after the bell. It wasn't the most devastating punch Tyson had ever thrown and came across as more of a petulant cheap shot than anything. He had two points deducted as the crowd booed Brownsville's most famous pantomime villain

Orlin Norris then went down on his back in delayed fashion

after the punch and then looked somewhat sheepish and got back up again to walk back to his corner. Tyson (now trained by Tommy Brooks) came out for the second to find Norris still on his stool.

Orlin Norris had quit, claiming a knee injury (which, to be fair to Orlin, was later verified) as a result of going down at the end of the first round. The fight was ruled no-contest and Tyson echoed the sentiments of everyone who had tuned in when he said "I'm tired of this s***." The Tyson camp felt that Norris and his corner were exaggerating the effect of the punch and the injury to get Orlin a DQ win - which would have led to a nice rematch payday.

Tyson's purse was temporarily withheld from the bout but then handed over when it proved impossible to ascertain whether the punch just after the bell was purposefully malicious. Orlin Norris and his management salivated at the expected rematch payday they would collect but Tyson decided to pull the rug out from under them and take his increasingly obstreperous act on the road.

Tyson announced (to the ire of Norris, who launched an unsuccessful legal challenge once he realised his rematch hopes were dust) that he would travel across the Atlantic to take on the British champion Julius Francis in Manchester. The fight with Francis made a lot of sense as British fans (and the generally curious) were eager to see Tyson in the flesh and so there was money to be made. It would also get Tyson out of the United States where the commissions were (understandably) starting to grow more than a little weary of the carnage and confusion he seemed to bring to any event.

The fight with Francis was a gross mismatch but no one could deny that the likeable 35 year-old Julius, a journeyman who

had lost seven fights since taking up boxing in his late twenties, at least deserved a decent twilight payday for all of his toil. Francis managed to get the Tyson fight through a three fight winning streak that brought victories over his domestic rivals Pele Reid, Scott Welch and Danny Williams.
Tyson's main concern was getting into the United kingdom to fight Francis. After protests and much debate, the British Home Secretary decided that Tyson should be allowed in to fight. Lest we forget, Tyson was a convicted rapist. There was much controversy about him fighting in Britain.

The Tyson v Francis fight was more of an event than a sporting contest. Julius enjoyed his fifteen minutes of fame and took up an offer to have the soles of his boxing shoes sponsored for £20,000.

Tyson was mobbed in Brixton (an area of London with a large black community) when he went out for a walk. Some found this distasteful given that he was a convicted rapist but it illustrated how he was one of the few boxers aside from Muhammad Ali who transcended the sport and was famous around the world.

The light-hitting Julius Francis lacked the power to keep Tyson at bay and was knocked down five times before the referee called a halt in the second round. The exercise in Manchester hadn't proved an awful lot in terms of Tyson's status as a contender but it did prove that he could draw a crowd in Europe.

Five months later Tyson was back in the United Kingdom to meet more protests as he took on the big Texan Lou Savarese in Glasgow. The pair were supposed to meet in Milan but when Tyson had to attend the funeral of a friend and needed more time to train the fight was postponed and moved to

Scotland.

Glasgow, like Manchester, was eager to see Tyson and there was plenty of money to made for Iron Mike and his British promoter Frank Warren. Only this time the trip took on the aura of a bad nightmare and ensured that Tyson would not fight in the British Isles again. Frank Warren, who had brought Tyson to Britain in the first place, sported an obvious eye injury at this time and there were heavy rumours that Tyson had been responsible after an altercation.

Frank Warren would later say that Tyson was like different people in the Francis and Savarese. Tyson had been cordial and easy to deal with for the Francis fight but in Glasgow he was sullen and unpredictable. Tyson was paid $8 million to fight Lou Savarese. He later admitted that he only trained two weeks for the fight.

Savarese seemed on the face of it to be a reasonable choice of opponent. He was 6'5 and had wins over Buster Mathis Jr and Lance Whitaker. He stopped the comebacking Buster Douglas in the first round of a 1998 fight and had gone the distance with George Foreman and Michael Grant in losses. At the very least he might test Tyson's stamina - which was even more suspect given Mike's lack of conditioning. Tyson arrived by Concorde for the Savarese fight and avoided the press at Heathrow airport.

Tyson was off the mood-altering prescription drug Zoloft for the Savarese fight and seemed like a man possessed at a rain sodden Hampden Park. Tyson later claimed in his autobiography that he was high when he entered the ring to fight Savarese and his crazed behaviour suggests he wasn't lying. By now Tyson was a habitual user of drugs but evaded being caught in drug tests by using someone else's urine.

Tyson went after Lou Savarese like a madman and dropped him with practically the first punch. When Savarese got up, Tyson went in for the kill and when the referee John Coyle tried to stop the fight Tyson seemed oblivious to him and carried on pounding away on Lou. Coyle was then knocked down himself in the confusion and had to jump again to try and stop the fight for a second time while the cornermen entered the ring to prize everyone apart. Even by the standards of Mike Tyson fights this was a crazy round of madness and confusion.

For his conduct in the Savarese fight, Tyson was retrospectively fined $187,500 by the British Boxing Board of Control for misconduct. He'd probably lost more than that down the back of his sofa. Not that the British Boxing Board of Control probably saw a penny of Tyson's money anyway.

The fight was over at 38 seconds of the first round and Tyson immediately began ranting at Lennox Lewis (now the unified champion after beating Evander Holyfield) when interviewed by Showtime. "I was gonna rip his heart out. I'm the best ever. I'm the most brutal and vicious, the most ruthless champion there has ever been. No one can stop me. Lennox is a conqueror? No! He's no Alexander! I'm Alexander! I'm the best ever. I'm Sonny Liston. I'm Jack Dempsey. There's never been anyone like me. I'm from their cloth. There is no one who can match me. My style is impetuous, my defense is impregnable, and I'm just ferocious. I want your heart! I want to eat his children! Praise to Allah."

Lennox Lewis didn't actually have any children at the time so it obviously would have been very difficult for Mike to eat them.

Jay Larkin, the Showtime senior vice president, demanded

that HBO 'release' Lennox Lewis so he could fight Tyson on Showtime. Mr Larkin was obviously being a trifle optimistic with this suggestion. Frank Maloney, the manager of Lennox Lewis, was not terribly impressed by all of this. "He's a carnival act now," said Maloney of Tyson. "That's all he is."

At this time Tyson was basically fighting for nothing. His purses were going to Showtime - who Tyson still owed $13 million because they bailed him out when he was bankrupted by a tax bill. Tyson had come out of prison owing the United States Inland Revenue Service $100 million. You can't help thinking that Bill Cayton would have avoided such a mess had he still been running Tyson's affairs.

Tyson sold two mansions, which netted $40 million, and then made about $50 million through his post-prison pay-per-view fights on Showtime. That left him owing about $10 million - which became $13 million due to him overspending on unnecessary luxuries like fashion brands, cars, and jewelry. It is little wonder Tyson was tired of fighting. He was basically having to go in the ring and fight just to break even.

"One minute I'm robbing a dope house," reflected a maudlin Tyson, musing on his past and rapid rise to fame. "Next minute I'm the youngest heavyweight champion of the world. I'm only 20, 19, with a lot of money. Who am I? What am I? I don't even know who I am. I'm just a dumb child who's being abused and robbed by lawyers. I'm just a dumb pugnacious fool. I'm just a fool who thinks he's someone. Then you tell me I should be responsible. I've been a prima-donna. I was taken care of since I was 13. That's why I am the way I am today. I was spoiled, like a brat. I had anything I wanted. That's crazy to be that way all your life. Everybody's taking care of you, but manipulating you at the same time. Very few people have a life like that. Most people have to work like slaves their whole lives. I've never had a job in my life. What I know how to do is hurt big, tough men — in the street and off."

Tyson's last fight of 2000 was much anticipated although probably not for the right reasons. His opponent would be Andrew Golota, the "Foul Pole" as the American boxing press sometimes dubbed him.

Golota was a huge white Polish heavyweight who shot to prominence when he twice battered Riddick Bowe and then threw victory away when he was disqualified for low-blows in the last rounds. All Golota had to do to beat Bowe was box his way through to the end but he seemed to have a self-destructive lack of discipline that reminded many of Tyson. Earlier in his career Golota had also, like Mike Tyson, bitten an opponent.

The prospect of Golota meeting Tyson had many anticipating a WWE style anything goes brawl. But Golota, despite his fearsome reputation, had a fragile psyche. He folded in one round in a 1997 title fight with Lennox Lewis and seemed to be beating overhyped prospect Michael Grant handily when he quit in the last round of a 1999 contest. His fight with Tyson at The Palace, Auburn Hills, Michigan, proved to be another bizarre night in the careers of both men.

Tyson came out fast in aggressive fashion and Golota immediately looked somewhat flustered and uncomfortable. Tyson looked better than he had done for a long time in the first round. He slipped punches and countered well. The old speed that the 1980s Tyson possessed in abundance was never going to return but at least he was showing some upper-body movement again at last.

Golota went down from a big right-hand and ended the round

with a cut. Golota would later claim that he was disoriented and injured after being butted - which was somewhat ironic given Tyson's complaints about Holyfield's head.

Despite his huge size advantage, Golota couldn't seem to get to grips with Tyson and looked like a novice golden glover trying to fend off the attacks. Between the second and third rounds Golota told his corner he didn't want to continue. His trainer Al Certo was gobsmacked and clearly furious.

Golota was jeered as he left the ring and his purse was withheld. Golota was branded a coward but those quick to judge had to take back their scorn when it was later established that he had suffered a concussion, a fractured left cheekbone, and a herniated disc.

What had been an impressive performance by Tyson in the Golota fight was scratched from TKO3 to No-Contest when he tested positive for marijuana. By this stage of his career no one was hugely surprised by anything that happened to him anymore. Tyson's boxing license in Michigan was suspended for three months.

The main goal for Tyson and his team in 2001 was to get a big money title fight with Lennox Lewis. The fight with Lewis would give Tyson, who was no spring chicken now, one big last blockbuster payday. If there was a Lewis rematch then he'd make even more money and might at last be able to clear his debts.

To this end, Tyson signed to fight top ten contender David Izon in May. But a sloppy Lennox Lewis didn't bother to train or travel early to acclimatise in a defence against Hasim Rahman in Johannesburg and was stopped in the fifth round.

Tyson and his manager Shelly Finkel lost interest in Izon and started to lobby for a fight with Rahman but Rahman was tied to a rematch clause with Lewis despite attempts by Don King to make a Rahman v Izon fight. It was quite a merry-go-round. The Rahman v Lewis rematch was set for November 2001 and in order to keep busy and earn more much needed money, Tyson and his team signed to fight the Danish fighter Brian Nielsen in Copenhagen on September the 8th.

While he began training for the Brian Nielsen fight, Tyson was accused of sexual assault in the California resort town of Big Bear City. Nothing came of the charges but it was another reminder of how trouble and suspicion seemed to dog him at every turn.

Despite his 62-1 record, Brian Nielsen was not taken very seriously by the boxing world at large. The pudgy Dane had fought geriatric names that had seen better days (Tim Witherspoon, Bonecrusher Smith, Tony Tubbs etc) and been the recipient of a highly questionable home advantage points decision over the ancient Larry Holmes in 1997.

There was too the farce of Brian Nielsen picking up the dubious IBO championship and gunning for Rocky Marciano's 49-0 record. It was all too comical for words and boxing historians everywhere were probably relieved or simply amused when an exhausted Nielson collapsed to a tenth round loss to someone called Dicky Ryan in the bout that was supposed to make history. Nielsen was so fatigued near the end of the Ryan fight he was staggering around the ring like some comedy drunk. You can see the (less than impartial) referee is clearly doing his level best to protect Nielsen, prop him up, and give him as many rests as possible.

There were even stories that some of Brian Nielsen's fights

had been fixed. Affidavits and related court documents in a 2004 boxing corruption investigation in Las Vegas claimed that boxing agent Robert Mittleman had 'bribed' Jeremy Williams with $10,000 and a Lincoln Navigator SUV to lose a March 21, 2000, bout in Denmark against Brian Nielsen. Williams then allegedly got $40,000 as well on top of that to throw the fight. Jeremy Williams was actually seen in a bar the night before he fought Nielsen so he wasn't exactly adhering to a monastic training regime.

A lot of Nielsen's fights seemed a bit dodgy. Tim Witherspoon never threw any right hands against the Dane and Tony Tubbs quit with an alleged leg injury. The punch which stopped Witherspoon seemed to go above his shoulder. It looked like Witherspoon was simply pretending to be hurt. Brian Nielsen's fight with Bonecrusher was ended when the Dane headbutted Bonecrusher - opening a large cut. Nielsen got no punishment for the butt though and was declared the victor on a TKO! Larry Holmes gave Nielsen a boxing lesson but then got jobbed by a hometown decision. Holmes later suggested he'd been poisoned too.

Brian Nielson had won thirteen straight since the embarrassing Ryan defeat but he was merely a fringe contender. He might scrape into a fallow thirty but that was about it. His marketability stemmed from him being a big fish in a small pond. All his fights were in Denmark against very carefully selected opposition. Tyson was by far the toughest fight he'd ever taken - even if this was not a prime Mike Tyson.

Tyson was paid $5 million to travel to Denmark to fight Nielson and he certainly lived it large, treating the trip as more of a holiday than anything serious. Come fight night, a grossly out of shape Tyson weighed in at a shade under 240 pounds. Neilson was even more bloated at a whopping 260 pounds.

The Tyson/Nielson fight had all the excitement and drama of a man fighting a paper bag. The 36 year-old Nielson ambled onto the ropes and allowed a patently out of condition Tyson to thump away at him as if the Dane was a heavybag. Brian Nielson, for all his faults, was at least tough and durable. Tyson threw the kitchen sink at him in the first couple of rounds but the Dane covered up and managed to survive.

A combination sent Nielson down in the third but the big European managed to clinch enough to give the crowd a few more rounds of increasingly desperate slow motion entertainment. Nielson, his left eye shut, retired on his stool at the end of the sixth round and Tyson was declared a TKO winner. Despite the fact the fight had been one-sided it wasn't a very impressive performance by Tyson. Tyson seemed slow and out of shape. His reflexes were not what they once were.

The fight with Nielson was comfortable for Iron Mike but it did once again illustrate that Tyson's stamina was now almost non-existent. Tyson had come out all guns blazing in the fight but when the big Danish boxer survived the early blitz it was noticeable that Tyson sooned slowed down. He was like a battery that hadn't been fully charged. Tyson could only fight at a good pace for one or two rounds now. After that he would slow down and throw single punches. The things which made Tyson so devastating in the past, his speed, stamina, combination punching and constant pressure, were no longer available to him.

Throughout this last up and down phase of Tyson's career there was a lot of talk about a Tyson v David Tua fight. It seemed like a natural. Two big punchers with similar styles.

Tua was desperate for the Tyson fight and called out Tyson more than once. Sure, it was the payday which motivated him but he was also convinced he could beat this faded version of Tyson. Tua v Tyson was a fight that could have been made from 1999 until the end of Tyson's career but it never happened in the end. The main reason it never happened is probably that Tyson's camp thought Tua was too dangerous. They didn't want to jepordise a title shot by fighting anyone TOO tough. The main problem Tyson would face in this fight was that by 2001 he didn't have the greatest stamina. That spells disaster against Tua - a fighter who carried his knockout power into the late rounds. Tua was short for a heavyweight at 5'10 but he was built like a tank and impossible to hurt. He had a truly great chin. Tua's was famous for his left-hook. He was a fearsome puncher when this signature hook landed.

Tua's weakness was that he could be outboxed. If you were managing Tua you'd much rather put him in the ring with an aggressive puncher than a slick mover. Tua wasn't exactly light on his feet and would plod after his opponents. Despite his short stature he could weigh as much as 250 in the ring. He was just a very powerful and bulky man - simply not very tall. Tua had a title shot against Lennox Lewis in 2000. Many actually tipped him to win the fight but he found the size, reach, and boxing ability of Lewis too much to cope with. Lewis won a lopsided decision. Tua never got another title shot. Two fights later he was outpointed by the slippery Chris Byrd. Tua had good wins against Michael Moorer and Fres Oquendo and fought a draw with his old rival Hasim Rahman but he was never a major factor in the division again.

A month later, Lennox Lewis regained his world title with a spectacular fourth round knockout of Hasim Rahman in their rematch. The decks were now clearing for Tyson versus Lewis in what was likely to be Tyson's last hurrah.

Tyson felt he still needed a few more tune ups before tangling with Lewis and announced a January, 2002 fight with Ray Mercer. Mercer was past his prime by 2002 but in the end Tyson and team decided that it would be foolish to risk the Lewis payday by taking other fights and axed the Mercer fight.

Despite the fact that Tyson looked dreadful against Nielson, Lewis v Tyson was projected to be the biggest fight in boxing history. Tyson's increasingly unstable and erratic behaviour was of course, distasteful as it was, a big part of the appeal. The fight was complicated to arrange because Lewis was with HBO and Tyson with Showtime and both networks were adamant they should have exclusive rights. In the end the money made everyone willing to compromise just enough to get the deal done. The networks would, in effect, share the fight.

At a press conference in New York to officially announce the fight Tyson strolled out on stage to wait for Lewis and then apparently tried to attack him when a bemused Lewis entered with a bodyguard who seemed to try and push Tyson back. Their respective entourages engaged in a mass brawl and somewhere in the midst of all the chaos Tyson bit Lewis on the leg. José Sulaimán, the dictator president of the WBC for life, was caught up in the mayhem and filed a $56m lawsuit against Mike Tyson and Lennox Lewis. Sulaimán said he had some teeth knocked out in the chaos. Shelly Finkel, Tyson's manager, was surprised when he learned of the lawsuit. He's said he'd have a lawyer look into it. Finkel was no fan of Sulaimán as Sulaimán and Don King had ripped off his former fighter Pernell Whitaker twice in famous high profile robberies.

The Lewis/Tyson fight was supposed to take place in Las Vegas but the Nevada State Athletic Commission voted 4-1 to deny Tyson a licence and it was Memphis that coughed up the big site fee to get the fight. Lewis and Tyson were to be paid a guaranteed $17.5 million. It was the highest-grossing event in pay-per-view history, generating $106.9 million from 1.95 million buys in the United States.

The paradox of this fight is that Lennox Lewis was the better fighter but Mike Tyson was the greater draw. Lewis needed Tyson more than Tyson needed Lewis. Lewis spoke of beating Tyson to secure his 'legacy' but that didn't really stand up to scrutiny. Mike Tyson's prime years were 1986-1988. Tyson was a good fourteen years removed from his prime when he fought Lennox Lewis.

Tyson had parted ways with trainer Tommy Brooks - allegedly over money. This seemed to be a mistake as Brooks had done a pretty decent job in getting the ageing fighter back to some sort of consistency. Brooks was replaced by Ronnie Shields - a former boxer and now respected trainer. Some boxing writers felt Shields should have taken a stand and refused to allow Panana Lewis to join Tyson's team but he did nothing of the sort. You could hardly blame Shields for not kicking up a fuss given that he was about to get a cut of Tyson's $17.5 million dollar payday.

Ronnie Shields, who is a thoughtful and likeable man, got on well with Tyson and watched a lot of old fight films with him. Shields later admitted that Tyson was well past his best when he trained him. Another member of 'Team Tyson' was Darryl Francis - now working as Mike's personal assistant. Darryl Francis had previously been convicted of assault. Francis was in charge of Tyson's logistics and was sometimes seen ferrying the fighter around in a Rolls-Royce.

Tyson didn't endear himself to anyone with his other team members for the Lewis fight, most notably Panama Lewis, a man forever shamed for the despicable and ultimately tragic act of removing the padding from the gloves of Luis Resto when he fought a young fighter named Billy Collins years ago. The depressed Collins never fought again after his doctored gloves pounding and died in a car crash not long afterwards. Panana Lewis had also been involved in a "mysterious bottle" incident when Aaron Pryor fought Alexis Arguello. It was alleged that Panama Lewis gave Pryor some illicit substance via his 'special bottle' between rounds to give him an advantage. Panama Lewis denied this accusation and said the bottle merely contained a mint drink to settle Pryor's upset stomach.

Tyson's other unloveable camp member was Steve "Crocodile" Fitch, an obnoxious cheerleader who wore combat fatigues and went around shouting a lot until everyone wanted to strangle him. Fitch was Mike Tyson's 'motivator-in-chief' - for which he was paid $150,000 a fight. No wonder Tyson was broke! Fitch had once served time in prison for manslaughter.

"Crocodile is back from the swamp," said Lennox Lewis' trainer Emanuel Steward. "And then they went to the swamp and got Panama Lewis. That's too bad because it brings things back in the direction of it being a freak show. We have a big enough problem with Mike's reputation and integrity without bringing in Panama Lewis. I don't want Panama Lewis or Crocodile anywhere near the ring on Saturday night because, when they realize that Mike is about to get knocked out, they could resort to anything."

Emanuel "Manny" Steward was born in Bottom Creek, West Virginia, in 1944. He moved to Detroit as a young man and worked in the auto industry. Steward began training at the Brewster Recreation Center and embarked a career as an amateur boxer, eventually winning 93 fights and losing only 3. It was as a trainer and mentor though that Steward became a legend. The Kronk gym in Detroit, housed in an old basement, was built into a home of champions by Steward. The gym for years was seen as a way to keep kids out of trouble and off the streets in southwestern Detroit. The Kronk gym was in the bowels of an old building, claustrophobic and unbearably hot from overhead pipes. Sparring sessions there were often better than any real fight.

Many famous fighters and champions were trained there by Steward - most famously Thomas Hearns. Thomas Hearns was one of the most popular, exciting and successful boxers of the modern era. He won several world titles in different weights and became one of the 'five kings' alongside Sugar Ray Leonard, Marvin Hagler, Roberto Duran and Wilfred Benitez - a clutch of great boxers who fought in a number of memorable bouts against one another and made up boxing's last golden age. When Hearns won the welterweight championship from Pipino Cuevas, the weight of the city of Detroit was literally on his shoulders that night and he gave the economically depressed city a huge lift when he won. Hilmer Kenty had already became Steward's first world champion in 1980 and there would be many more to come.

Detroit had put the United States 'on wheels' after World War 2 in the auto-boom but car production peaked in 1955 only to be followed by a recession that put 20% of the workforce out of a job. Major firms like Packard, Hudson, and Studebaker closed down. Poor black migrants like the Hearns family then settled into areas that looked like war zones. When Hearns became a superstar boxer he gave the city something to be proud of again and even in the twilight of his career could still draw a big crowd in his home town. Steward and the Kronk gym gave hope and pride to Detroit.

Steward was a wise, generous, and kind man who formed a parental bond with his boxers and would even cook their meals. From the moment the contracts were signed to the moment the last bell rang, Kronk fighters could always be sure that Emanuel Steward had their back and would look after them. The success of the Kronk gym was a great source of inspiration to the people of Detroit - especially poor black kids who were interested in becoming boxers themselves. Steward would go on to be a successful trainer for many years. He resurrected the career of Lennox Lewis and turned him into the undisputed heavyweight champion and also worked wonders for Wladimir Klitschko.

The dignified and classy team of Lennox Lewis and Manny Steward were a stark contrast indeed to Mike Tyson, "Crocodile" Fitch, and Panama Lewis. Emanuel Steward who made the technical modifications to Lennox Lewis that brought him so much success in the last phase of boxing life. Steward said the incredible thing about Lewis was that despite being 250 pounds and 6'6 he was still an athlete. It was rare for someone so huge to be co-ordinated and skillful.

Lennox Lewis was famous for his love of chess and often pictured over the chessboard in his training camps but this used to irritate Steward. He felt Lewis was like a chess player in the ring far too often and always felt the boxer should eschew his more analytical safety first instincts and be more ruthless. Lennox Lewis was a pretty classy champion and cut a striking figure with his suits and dreadlocks. He was never in any trouble outside the ring, well spoken, reserved and private. While other fighters got drunk outside the ring Lewis drank tea and avoided the limelight. He liked the quiet life.

Maybe this was why he never seemed to get the credit he deserved from the American press. They thought Lewis was dull.

Tyson's bizarre behaviour before the Lewis fight reached new disturbing lows when he overheard a journalist suggest he should be put in a straightjacket and launched into a profanity laced tirade while appearing to be on the cusp of tears. His interviews in training camp were frequently obscene and incoherent. Tyson seemed to be in meltdown.

Strange as it seems in hindsight, Lewis was only a 2-1 favourite and many liked the chances of a Tyson victory. They were blinded by nostalgia rather than guided by cold logic.

In reality, all Lennox had to do was get through the first round or two and Mike would be a busted flush. It was doubtful that Tyson could fight several hard competitive rounds with a powerful heavyweight like Lennox Lewis now. One can see in the early 2000s version of Tyson is desperate to get rid of opponents early because he knows full well that he doesn't have the gas tank anymore for long fights.

Paradoxically, while Tyson was arguably 15 years removed from his prime, Lewis had been a late bloomer and at 35 seemed to be as good as ever. The Tyson-esque New Zealand slugger David Tua had failed to land a glove on Lewis in their title fight a few years before so it was hard to see how Tyson, at this advanced stage of his career, was likely to do much better.

There was fear the arena would be half empty due to overpriced tickets but they manage to sell most of them in the end. Tyson and Lewis did not do much to promote the fight once they arrived in Memphis. Tyson skipped a press conference while Lennox Lewis kept a low profile. The focus of Lewis was the fight. He didn't care about the hype and promotion.

Mike Tyson made his way to ring with gangsta rap. Bob Marley was the sonic backdrop for the ring walk of Lewis. Come fight night Lewis and Tyson were separated in the by yellow jacketed security guards lest there should be any last minute Tyson shenanigans. There was no staredown - the boxers getting their instructions in the dressing room beforehand.

Tyson (lighter than in was in Denmark but still looking overweight at 234) started fast, looking for an early kayo but Lewis was calm and tied the shorter man up before hammering in some uppercuts to show he wouldn't be bullied. Tyson moved his head in the first round but stopped doing it thereafter. He missed wildly with a hook and Lewis leaned down on Tyson, using his greater weight and strength. Tyson showed a flash of the old Tyson with a hook off the jab but Lewis landed a right late in the round as Tyson stooped low. It was a fairly even round but Tyson's attacking intent meant he probably deserved it by a whisker. "If you see how bad he looks you'd be surprised," Steward told Lewis in the corner.

Lewis landed a big uppercut early in the second and started to get his jab working. Lewis was also using his strength to shove Tyson back - similar to the tactics Evander Holyfield had used to negate Tyson's offensive style. Lewis was warned by the referee Eddie Cotton for holding but he was also starting to time the oncoming Tyson with uppercuts. Tyson couldn't get inside and close the distance and as the pace lulled Lewis began to dominate from the outside.

In the third Lewis began to move more and outboxed Tyson from the outside. Tyson look discouraged although he did manage a flurry that had the crowd excited for a fleeting moment. But a jab cuts Tyson above the eye and his night becomes even more difficult.

As the fourth round began, blood was visible on Tyson's face. Lewis landed a thumping right and started to impose himself more and more. He shoved Tyson back and landed a left-hook to the body as Iron Mike began to bleed from the nose. Lewis seemed to knock Tyson down with a right-hand but the referee Eddie Cotton ruled that Lewis had pushed him down as a toppling Tyson leaned forwards. Bizarrely, Cotton then took a point from a bemused Lewis.

After a brief surge from Tyson at the start of the fifth it was all Lewis again. Lewis seemed to hurt Tyson with a right-hook inside but Eddie Cotton warned him for hitting and holding and gave Tyson time to recover. Cotton, for reasons best known to himself, seems to be doing all he can to help Tyson in the fight. Larry Merchant on HBO acidly comments that Lennox is fighting both Tyson and the referee.

Lewis pot shots with the jab when they continue and at the bell Tyson's trainer Ronnie Shields implores him to throw more punches. But the sixth and seventh round are one-way traffic as Lewis starts to line up a patently exhausted Tyson with the right-hand and hit him at will. There is something glum and listless about Tyson in the Lewis fight. It is as if he knew he couldn't win.

Tyson came out fast in the eighth and threw a couple of thudding rights at the side of Lewis but it's too late. He walks onto a combination and his knees buckle. Eddie Cotton (erroneously) gives him a count and the end is nigh. A big slashing right ends the contest and Tyson fails to beat the ten count. It was - ultimately - a brutal mismatch and the most punishing defeat of Tyson's career. For those who remembered the young Mike Tyson from the 1980s it was depressing to watch him in the Lewis fight. 'Tyson has long been a shell of his former self, propped up by investors who want their end back,' wrote the Boxing Chronicle. 'Perhaps the only surprise for Tyson-watchers was that he fought within the rules and didn't quit on his stool.'

Tyson, as chaotic as the pre-fight nonsense had been, emerged with some respect from the last big blockbuster pay-per-view event of his career. He had taken his beating like a man and after the fight he even displayed his tender side when he praised Lewis and wiped some blood from the face of his opponent. It was a small moment but a reminder of what a puzzle Tyson was. For a second he could have been the young teenage Tyson who would be polite and respectful and talk excitedly about old fight films. "Mike Tyson fought a very courageous fight tonight," said Tyson's trainer Ronnie Shields. "He gave the best he could. I don't know what he is going to do now."

Lewis was eager for a rematch for two salient reasons. (1) He knew he would win again and (2) it would be a big payday to take into retirement. Tyson needed the rematch fo financial reasons but somehow he eventually let it slip from his grasp. He said he needed some tune-ups before he boxed Lewis again but at nearly 36 it was probably not going to make much difference.

Tyson divorced his wife Monica Turner in 2003 and filed for bankruptcy. Tyson's days of commanding huge fight purses were almost over so things looked bleak indeed. Tyson would later marry his third (and at the time of writing last) wife

Lakiha Spicer in 2009. He would have seven children in all.

# CHAPTER FIVE (2003 - 2024)

In February, 2003, Tyson was back in Memphis with new trainer Freddie Roach to fight Clifford "The Black Rhino" Etienne for $5 million and speculation arose that if Tyson won then a summer rematch with Lewis might go ahead. Lewis had given Tyson a deadline to accept a summer rematch. Tyson insisted though that he needed tune up fights.

It was rather difficult to see how anyone could sell a Lewis/Tyson rematch given the one-sided nature of the first fight. In the end though, Lewis, who was 37 and nearing retirement, lost patience and moved on. Lewis sued Tyson for $20 million for bailing out on his rematch promise. Lennox would have the join the long que of people asking Mike for money.

Clifford Etienne began boxing late after time in prison and was a real prospect at one time after wins against Lamon Brewster and Lawrence Clay Bey but a loss to Fres Oquendo that saw Etienne down seven times had derailed his progress and introduced some realism into projections of how far he might go. In his only fight of note since then he had drawn with Tyson's old foe Frans Botha.

At 225, Tyson looked trimmer than he had done for a while but it was of course impossible to know if training or drugs had made him so fashionably slender. The fight lasted 49 seconds and Etienne's performance evoked memories of Bruce Seldon's meek surrender to Tyson in the nineties. Etienne went down from the first solid punch that Tyson landed and while prostrate on the canvas seemed aware enough to take his gumshield out before resuming his prostrate form again like an actor playing a death scene on the stage. Maybe Etienne just thought better of getting walloped again.

After the fight with Clifford Etienne, Tyson did not get back in the ring for 17 months. His life was in a crazy freefall. Tyson nearly signed to fight Oleg Maskaev on the undercard of Lennox Lewis' June title defence against Vitali Klitschko but legal troubles (alleged to come from Don King) scuppered the plan. It would have paved the way for Lewis v Tyson 2.

2003 was the year that Bill Cayton died. He was 85. After his business relationship with Mike Tyson ended, Cayton had managed other fighters - most notably Tommy Morrison and Vinnie Pazienza (or Vinnie Paz). Cayton also sold his fight film library to Disney in 1998. Disney owned the ESPN Classic network and hired Cayton as the boxing coordinator for ESPN2's Friday Night Fights show. Bill Cayton had lived long enough to see Mike Tyson's life, finances, and boxing career implode.

Mike Tyson didn't really have anything to say about Cayton's passing. Bill Cayton did a few interviews after Mike Tyson left him. Cayton simply said he felt sorry for Mike that his boxing career and finances never quite panned out the way they should have done. Cayton said he ranked the young Mike Tyson (the one who knocked out Spinks in 90 seconds) as the second greatest heavyweight of all time after Ali. Needless to say, Bill felt that Mike's potential had been ruined by him taking up with Don King.

Tyson's 2003 rapidly descended into cocaine madness. He got into trouble for beating up two autograph hunters and kicked

Don King in the head during some vague attempt at settling the circuitous legal maze their association had created. Tyson was also accused of breaking a bone in the face of one of King's bodyguards - which led to a lawsuit. The Don King bodyguard suing Tyson was 44 year-old Isadore "Izzy" Bolton. Bolton said that Tyson dragged him out of a car and punched him twice - leaving him with blurred vision. In June, Tyson had also been arrested for punching two men in a hotel. Tyson seemed to have temporarily lost his ability to distinguish real life from the boxing ring.

A maudlin Tyson bared his soul in an interview relating to his financial woes - although it was rather hard to feel too sorry for a man who had blown $300 million by treating it like monopoly money. "I've got nowhere to live," said Tyson. "I've been crashing with friends, literally sleeping in shelters. Unsavoury characters are giving me money and I'm taking it. I need it. The drug dealers, they sympathise with me. They see me as some sort of pathetic character ... I know I was a tough, bad-ass talking fighter, but I ain't no mob figure. I did my time for the rape. I paid my money to Las Vegas. I paid my dues. I ain't the same person I was when I bit that guy's ear off."

Tyson said he had experienced the top of life and the gutter of life but he wanted to live in the 'middle' of life. The only problem was that he had no idea how to do that. Tyson just wanted to be a normal person after years of fame and craziness. Budd Schulberg had once wrote of Mike Tyson - 'It was Tyson against Tyson, a contest he had been fighting and losing ever since D'Amato got off at his final stop on life's subway years ago.' That quote seem more apt than ever.

In his bankruptcy declaration, Tyson said he owed $27 million. A chunk of that was to the Internal Revenue Service. He also owed money to a limousine company ($308,749); a Las

Vegas jeweler ($173,706); a New York rug store ($78,000); Ferrari of Beverly Hills ($60,603); and a Hawaiian resort ($30,000). Tyson also STILL owed money to ex-wife Robin Givens plus assorted lawyers, doctors, and managers. The obvious problem for Tyson now was that he was nearly 38 years-old and washed up as a fighter. In the past a $27 million debt could have been easily cleared with a big fight or two.

In July 2004, Tyson was finally back in the ring, this time in Louisville, Kentucky, to fight the unheralded 31-year-old British heavyweight Danny Williams. The heavyweight landscape had changed a lot and it was difficult to see how exactly Tyson fit in now. Lennox Lewis was retired and Evander Holyfield was now an oft-beaten gatekeeper - so fights with those two were no longer feasible. A fight between Tyson and Roy Jones Jr had often been mooted but Jones Jr was knocked out in the second round by Antonio Tarver in a May 2004 fight.

The dominant heavyweight now was the powerful 6'7 Ukrainian fighter Vitali Klitschko. The 38 year-old Tyson stood little chance of beating Klitschko. There was perhaps though the option of a fight with the volatile and crafty James Toney - who was now campaigning at heavyweight and doing surprisingly well. A press conference featuring Tyson and Toney would have been a trash talking classic. All of this speculation was academic though until Tyson had beaten Danny Williams.

Danny Williams was known as a wholehearted and competent fighter at domestic level in the United Kingdom but he had losses to Julius Francis and Michael Sprott on his record so Tyson, forgivably perhaps, wasn't taking him too seriously. Williams was installed as a 9-1 underdog against Tyson. Danny Williams was only chosen as the opponent because he was deemed no threat.

The Tyson v Danny Williams fight was promoted by a man named Chris Webb. Webb, who was unknown in boxing, was a former male stripper. Webb sold 17,000 tickets and managed to get a lot of television companies around the world to buy the fight. Tyson was faded but still had a big name. Chris Webb, who was 33, had a dodgy history according to reports - with allegations of inappropriate conduct with women. He also owed a lot of tax.

Chris Webb had promised Danny Williams $150,000. However, even on fight night Danny hadn't got a penny of this money. Frank Warren, the promoter of Danny Williams, was furious. Webb said he'd run out of money to pay Danny. Warren promised Danny he'd pay him his purse out of his own pocket and then managed to get $50,000 off Webb. After the fight Frank Warren took legal action against Chris Webb.

Straight-Out Promotions, the company of Chris Webb, then sued Frank Warren back, saying they had overpaid Warren. Webb also insisted that his company had a right to promote Danny Williams' next fight and take 50% of Danny's earnings! All of this confusion and bickering was par for the course in the crazy world of boxing. Tyson earned about $8 million for fighting Danny Williams. This is where all Chris webb's money went. Tyson was only expected to keep a small part of his purse - most of it would go to his creditors.

Tyson said in his autobiography that he took drugs right before fighting Danny Williams. Drugs or no drugs, Tyson nearly stopped Danny Williams in the first. He landed some stinging punches and had the huge Londoner (all 265 pounds of him) wobbling and disorganised. This was a familiar pattern with late era Tyson. He went all out to end the fight early because he knew he didn't have the conditioning for a longer fight.

Tyson however had torn a knee ligament through his exertions and a composed and determined Williams began to get on top, using his huge bulk to lean on Tyson and wear him down. It is almost impossible for fighters to win if they have a leg injury because it is through the legs that they plant themselves to generate power. Tyson was cut in the third from a stray elbow and received a low-blow. Danny Williams had two points deducted for the fouls but the end for Tyson was not far off anyway.

Mike Tyson's fighting spirit, sapped by years of abusing his body, seemed to wilt in the fourth. Williams began to pound Tyson with damaging punches and one could see that Tyson's stomach for combat had gone now after so many years in the squared circle. With his head completely shaved, the bald-pated Tyson looked like an old man against Williams.

Tyson went down and looked completely exhausted. He failed to clamber up in time and Williams began to celebrate. Danny Williams wouldn't have lasted a round against the 1986 version of Tyson but that version of Mike Tyson only existed in fight films and scrapbooks now. It was the end of an era.

It has long been a sad tradition in boxing that great fighters and champions inevitably end careers losing to people they would have demolished in their prime. One thinks of Roy Jones Jr fighting on long after he should have retired and being knocked out by men he would have once beaten with one arm tied behind his back. Danny Williams was gracious enough to later concede that he'd beaten an 'old Tyson' - not the real Mike Tyson. Danny said that Tyson punched very hard but he knew he would win when he started to push

Tyson back and realised that Mike was already getting tired. Williams had planned to box and use his jab in the first part of the fight but when he deduced that Tyson was tiring and becoming discouraged he decided to simply make the fight a brawl.

After the fight, Tyson's manager Shelly Finkel said that Mike still had plenty to offer and would fight again. That felt like a rather unrealistic assessment of the fight.

Tyson's trainer Freddie Roach was more humane in his assessment and suggested that Mike should be thinking about retirement. "He's in the hole a little bit," said Roach, "so he needs to fight. But I care about him as a person. I care for his health. What good is all the money in the world if you can't count it?" Showtime's Ken Hershman said that it was going to take some work to make Tyson a big pay-per-view attraction again. That was an understatement to say the least. If he couldn't beat Danny Williams then there wasn't much point in Tyson carrying on.

As a reward for beating Tyson, Danny Williams got a WBC title shot againt Vitali Klitschko. Danny was completely destroyed by Klitschko. It was a stark reminder of how faded Mike Tyson was and how far he now resided from the top heavyweights.

Tyson had knee ligament surgery after the Williams fight. His boxing future was uncertain. Shelly Finkel was right in saying that Tyson might well have stopped Danny Williams if he hadn't injured his knee but even if Tyson had won where he have gone next? Would he have gone after Klitschko and got a beating? Other alphabet titlists of this era like Chris Byrd and John Ruiz would have been favoured over Tyson too - and neither could draw flies so it isn't as if Tyson would have got a blockbuster payday anyway. Around this time, the promoter

Chris Webb talked about Tyson having a mixed martial arts fight with Bob "The Beast" Sapp in Japan. This never transpired (mercifully).

Mike Tyson would have one more fight in June 2005 at the at MCI Center in Washington. His opponent was a little known 32 year-old Irish heavyweight named Kevin McBride. McBride's 32-4-1 record included stoppage losses to Michael Murray, Louis Monaco, Axel Schulz and DaVarryl Williamson. He was the type of opponent the young Tyson would have feasted on in spectacular fashion but the fight would finally confirm that Tyson had absolutely nothing left.

Tyson got $5.5 million for the McBride fight. He only got $250,000 of that though after his creditors had taken their slice. Freddie Roach had parted ways with Tyson by now and so Mike was being trained by his friend Jeff Fenech. Jeff Fenech was a great Australian boxer who had fairly recently retired. Fenech and Tyson had been friends for a long time and fought on same of the same cards.

Tyson trained fairly well for the McBride fight - although he did vanish a few times. Fenech said that Mike was sparring for six rounds at a time and was showing some of his old head movement and combination punching. We had heard this before from later Tyson trainers and given that Mike was nearly 40 and had been inactive it was to be taken with a pinch of salt. It was presumed though that even an old and rusty Tyson would beat Kevin McBride.

Kevin McBride, who had been fighting in obscurity on ESPN, was paid $150,000 to fight Tyson. McBride's team, well aware of the trouble Danny Williams encountered getting his money when he fought Tyson, made sure that Kevin had the money in the bank BEFORE he got in the ring. There was a 20,000 crowd on fight night. The vast majority of them had come to watch and support Tyson. McBride was booed and the bagpipes which carried him to the ring were drowned out.

The Tyson/McBride bout featured more fouling and shoving than punching and Tyson - obviously out of condition and in no state to be in a boxing ring - was penalised for a head-butt. Tyson's old desperate trick of trying to twist his opponent's arm was also back. It was desperate stuff. Kevin McBride, like Danny Williams, was honest enough to later admit this was not exactly a prime Mike Tyson. The 1986 version of Mike Tyson would have beaten Danny Williams and Kevin McBride on the same night. Williams and McBride would have been lucky to last a couple of rounds with the 1996 version of Tyson let alone the 1986 one.

McBride, who weighed a preposterous 271 pounds, weathered the rough stuff and took Tyson's best shots when the faded slugger could land one. Tyson's handspeed was so diminished now that even his vaunted power seemed absent. Kevin McBride copied many of the tactics that Danny Williams used against Tyson - chiefly using his weight to lean down on Tyson and tire out the older man.

Kevin McBride said he could feel the energy sapping out of Tyson all the time. Mike simply didn't have the ability to fight hard anymore for more than a couple of rounds.

The last hurrah for Mike Tyson was the fourth. In this round he landed a couple of shots and seemed to have McBride discomforted. The big Irish boxer, all 6'7 of him, got through the round though and seemed to be getting stronger as Mike got weaker.

At the end of the sixth, Tyson was shoved to the canvas and

looked incapable of getting back up. He was on the verge of exhaustion. He retired on his stool before the seventh round and Kevin McBride had a victory, albeit a hollow largely meaningless one, over the worn out shell of what had once been one of the most exciting heavyweights to ever climb between the ropes.

"I don't have the guts to stay in the sport anymore," Tyson said after the McBride fight. "I most likely won't fight anymore. I won't disrespect the sport by losing to a fighter of this calibre." Two fights after beating Tyson, Kevin McBride was knocked out in the second round by Mike Mollo. McBride then lost five of his next six fights before retiring. The fact that Tyson had lost to McBride was all the evidence Mike needed that it was time to do something else. Sixteen days later Tyson announced his retirement.

Because of the vast potential he displayed as a teenage prodigy, Tyson is widely regarded to be an underachiever who possibly blew a chance to be one of the greatest heavyweights of all time. Wherever one places him in the pantheon of heavyweight history it is fair to say that very few boxers have ever generated the same amount of excitement and intrigue. Boxing does not occupy the same position in the mainstream that it once did decades ago. It's a niche sport now, one that rarely grabs the headlines. When Tyson was around, for better or worse, that was never the case.

The fighter that Tyson was often compared to, both in and out of the ring, was Sonny Liston. Charles 'Sonny' Liston was, for a brief time, the most feared man in boxing and the world heavyweight champion in the early sixties. Liston was considered unstoppable, a big hulking ex-convict with shoulders that could probably hold up a bridge and a baleful stare that terrified opponents before the bell even rang. When he demolished liberal establishment darling Floyd Patterson to become champion, Liston soon realised he was never going to be loved or accepted by anyone, neither black or (especially) white. Liston then lost twice to a brash young boxer by the name of Cassius Clay/Muhammad Ali (two fights that remain controversial to this day because of the endings and Liston's mob connected owners) and gradually faded away from the limelight. He was found dead in 1971, apparently the victim of a drug overdose although his widow maintained he had a phobia of needles.

Tyson (who was frequently compared to Liston both in the ring and out of it) was famous for visiting Liston's grave with flowers and watching videos of him working out to 'Night Train' (a jazz song written by Jimmy Forrest that Liston loved). Like Liston, many predicted that Tyson would likely end up in a premature grave.

In 2006, Tyson, desperately in need of money, re-entered the ring for a series of four-round boxing exhibitions called Mike Tyson's World Tour. Tyson, wearing a white shirt to his his obvious bulk, sparred with journeyman Corey "T-Rex" Sanders in the exhibitions. It wasn't quite Joe Louis having to turn to wrestling for money but it was a somewhat sad spectacle for those who remembered the young Tyson nonetheless.

Tyson, now aged 40, actually looked sharper and more dangerous against Corey "T-Rex" Sanders than he had done in his last professional fight. It was though just an exhibition so nothing much could be gleaned from it. There was talk that Tyson was using the exhibition tour to sharpen up so that he could make a real comeback to the boxing ring. He desperately needed money.

"If I don't get out of this financial quagmire there's a possibility I may have to be a punching bag for somebody. The money I make isn't going to help my bills from a tremendous standpoint, but I'm going to feel better about myself. I'm not going to be depressed," said Tyson. The problem with the suggestion that Tyson might launch a real comeback off the back of an exhibition is that exhibitions, training, and sparring are not true barometers of where a fighter is. It is only in a real fight, with an opponent punching back, that a fighter's punch resistance and conditioning can be truly tested.

Mike Tyson's World Tour was scrapped after one bout through lack of interest. That's the problem with exhibition bouts. No one wants to watch a 'pretend' fight. Near the end of 2006, Tyson was pulled over by the police with three bags of cocaine in his possession. He received 24 hours in jail and three years' probation the following year.

In 2008, a documentary about Tyson premiered in Cannes and showed that the public's fascination with Tyson was still there. "Tyson: The Movie" was directed by James Toback. The film was 90 minutes long and consisted mostly of Tyson alone talking directly to the camera with archive footage, split-screens and arty shots of a silhouetted Tyson gazing out to sea on a beach at sunset. It was an interesting insight into the former boxer although he later admitted he was rather drug addled at the time.

Tyson chokes up remembering Cus D'Amato in the documentary and we see footage of him eating dinner with his late mentor. His former managers Jim Jacobs and Bill Cayton are "slavemasters" although he seems philosophical about his short-lived and acrimonious marriage to Head of the Class actress Robin Givens. "We were just kids," shrugs Tyson.

It doesn't come as a huge shock to hear Tyson deny that he raped Desiree Washington in the documentary. The lack of any other perspective makes the film a one-sided account and here this approach becomes something of a weakness. He calls Washington a "swine". Tyson's recollections of his sexual exploits and general attitude to women is rather grim in the documentary.

There is some footage of the teenage Tyson washing dishes and eating dinner at D'Amato's house with other boxers and guests and you get a sense that Tyson is tearfully nostalgic about those days because it was the last time his life was ever normal and D'Amato was the last man he ever really trusted. Tyson almost chuckles when he pictures the scene. A young black street kid from Brownsville suddenly living with all these white people Waltons style in leafy Catskill.

Tyson's explanation for his meltdown against Evander Holyfield - which left a part of The Real Deal's ear in Tyson's mouth - was that he was about to blackout from Holyfield's constant headbutts. He reverted to the young Tyson on the streets of Brownsville and turned it into a streetfight. He just didn't care anymore. Perhaps the most harrowing footage in the film is a clearly unstable Tyson launching into an obscene tirade at a beery fan who has heckled him during a press event.

The documentary isn't particularly cinematic in the manner that When We Were Kings was - and that film was understandably more uplifting than 'Tyson' with Muhammad Ali as its central subject - but there are some great montages of the young Tyson tearing his way through a generation of heavyweights - Spinks, Biggs, Tubbs, Holmes, Berbick, Thomas - in spectacular fashion in addition to many of his brutal early knockouts and mismatches. It reminds you of what an incredible force of nature the young Tyson was.

Footage of his last couple of fights when Tyson had been stripped of his physique, speed and menacing aura and is only fighting for money makes for a sharp contrast. The film is at its best and most compelling though when Tyson talks about boxing and what it is like to climb into the squared circle - "I'm afraid. I'm afraid of everything. I'm afraid of losing. I'm afraid of being humiliated. But I'm confident. The closer I get to the ring the more confident I get. The closer, the more confident. The closer the more confident I get. All during training I've been afraid of this man. I think this man might be capable of beating me. I've dreamed of him beating me. For that I've always stayed afraid of him. The closer I get to the ring the more confident I get. Once I'm in the ring I'm a god. No one can beat me."

Tyson suffered a personal tragedy in 2009 with the accidental death of his four year-old daughter Exodus. Soon after he married Lakiha Spicer and tried to put his crazy life behind him in tribute to Exodus

Tyson had done a few small acting jobs over the years and a bit part in The Hangover led to appearances in the sequels and renewed interest in him. In 2010 he said - "I'm totally destitute and broke. But I have an awesome life, I have an awesome wife who cares about me. I'm totally broke. I had a lot of fun. It (poverty) just happened. I'm very grateful. I don't deserve to have the wife that I have; I don't deserve the kids that I have, but I do, and I'm very grateful."

They say there are no second acts in American life but that wasn't the case with Mike Tyson. Most people presumed he'd probably end up back in prison, but Tyson turned out to be a lot smarter than anyone suspected. He traded on his celebrity to carve out a new career. He even managed to repair his finances and get in the black again.

In 2011, Mike Tyson was inducted into the Boxing Hall of Fame in Canastota. Tyson was so moved by being inducted into the Boxing Hall of Fame that he couldn't finish his speech. He gave a mention to Bobby Stewart and Cus D'Amato - without whom he probably wouldn't have become a famous boxer.

In 2012, Tyson began a one-man show called Mike Tyson: Undisputed Truth. Mike Tyson: Undisputed Truth began in Las Vegas and moved to Broadway. Spike Lee even directed it. Mike Tyson: Undisputed Truth displayed a hitherto untapped resource in Mike Tyson - humour. Tyson was funny and self-deprecating on stage as he talked about the ups and downs of his crazy life.

Robin Givens, Cus, Evander Holyfield and more featured in Tyson's stage monologue. And of course Don King. Tyson said he eventually found out that King was charging him $8,000 a week for towels. You couldn't help but laugh really.

Mike Tyson: Undisputed Truth eventually led to a bestselling warts and all autobiography. Tyson autobiography was disappointing to some because, despite clocking in at 600 pages, it rather glossed over his boxing career and spent more time talking about all the women he'd slept with!

In 2014 a show called Mike Tyson Mysteries was launched. Mike Tyson Mysteries is an animated television series that premiered on Adult Swim in 2014. The show follows Mike Tyson, along with his eccentric team of mystery solvers including a talking pigeon, a ghost, and Tyson's adopted daughter, as they solve bizarre and comedic mysteries. The show blends elements of mystery, comedy, and absurdity,

Tyson has also ventured into the world of cannabis business, launching his own line of marijuana products called Tyson Ranch. He has also dabbled in cryptocurrency with the launch of his own Bitcoin wallet.

Tyson's acting career has seen him appear in a Law and Order spin-off, Ip Man 3, Scary Movie 5 and numerous VOD and foreign films. Tyson also launched a podcast called "Hotboxin' with Mike Tyson" where he interviews various guests and discusses a wide range of topics including sports, entertainment, and current events.

It is perhaps strange that, in an age of cancel culture, Mike Tyson has become what could you could even describe as a modestly beloved celebrity in American life. Tyson is (whatever he might say) a convicted rapist. Tyson once said he had done worse things than what he was alleged to have done to Desiree Washington. He said he left some things out of his autobiography to protect himself.

Don King continued to be the premier boxing promoter after Tyson left him in the late 1990s. He promoted Evander Holyfield for a time and also staged huge fights with the Puerto Rican superstar Felix Trinidad. In the end though King lost his grip on boxing and faded into irrelevance - despite still promoting a few fighters here and there. A lot of this was down to age. King was replaced by a new generation of promoters and boxing kingpins. People like Al Haymon and Eddie Hearn. King's old nemesis Bob Arum fared better though and continued to be relevant in the boxing world.

At a Boxing Hall of Fame event in 2018, Mike Tyson threw a glass of water at the 88 year-old King when Don tapped Tyson on the shoulder as if they were old friends. "He talked in there like he was my friend and that was just bullcrap," said Tyson. "He really did me in."

Tyson's old trainer Kevin Rooney is still in the Catskills training boxers. He never had a big name fighter after Tyson (unless you count Vinnie Paz) but continued to work. Rooney barely got a mention in Tyson's autobiography. Most people feel that Tyson was the never the same after leaving Rooney.

Tyson's amateur trainer Teddy Atlas later guided Michael Moorer to the heavyweight championship. Atlas trained many other top fighters like Timothy Bradley. He also worked as a boxing commentator and now has a successful podcast. Teddy Atlas did just fine without Mike Tyson.

In 2013, Tyson had encountered Teddy Atlas following his promotional debut on ESPN Friday Night Fights. This was the first time they had met since Atlas put a gun to his head all those years ago. Tyson apologised to Atlas and hugged him. "Maybe it was overwhelming to Teddy and he didn't get it yet," said Tyson. "But he has to know this is sincere. I don't wanna fight you no more. I was wrong. I'm sorry. I was wrong. I just wanted to make my amends. If he accepted it or not, at least I could die and go to my grave and say I made my amends with everybody I hurt. It's all about love and forgiveness, and in order to for those guys to forgive me -- other guys, you know, I want people to forgive the things I've done."

In 2020, Mike Tyson said he had been going to the gym and wanted to box some exhibitions for charity. Martial arts fighter Rafael Cordeiro was chosen to be Tyson's coach.

Tyson had no shortage of offers for his proposed exhibition

fight. He turned down $20 million from the Bare Knuckle Fighting Championship to fight an opponent of their choice. Tyson also  rejected an offer of $3 million from Australia to fight the rugby player/boxer Sonny Bill Williams.

Boston Boxing Promotions offered Tyson $1 million to fight a rematch with Peter McNeeley - another offer which was rejected. One person who angled to be Tyson's exhibition opponent was Evander Holyfield - who was now 57. Tyson set up a company to arrange the fight but a deal could not be reached with Holyfield. In the end a new opponent was found in Roy Jones Jr. Roy Jones was 51 and had only had his last real fight a few years before.

Tyson and Jones would fight eight two minutes rounds. The referee was told to stop the fight if it went 'beyond' an exhibition. The fight took place at the Staples Center, Los Angeles, on the 28th of November 2020. Former World Champions Chad Dawson, Kristy Dawson and Vinny Pazienza were the judges. The fight sold over 1.6 million PPV buys and generated over $80 million in revenue.

The fight itself, as you might expect, was a fairly slow paced affair. A pudgy Roy Jones Jr moved backwards and flicked out jabs. He would tie Mike up in close. Tyson looked a lot more threatening than Roy Jones Jr and landed some thumps to the body. It appeared as if Tyson was holding back somewhat. Had it been a real fight one suspects that Tyson would have overpowered Jones. The fight went the full eight rounds. Most people had Tyson winning comfortably but an eccentric score by judge Vinnie Paz earned Roy Jones Jr a draw.

The undercard featured Jake Paul. Jake Paul is an American YouTuber, internet personality, actor, and professional boxer. He first gained fame on the now-defunct app Vine, and later became known for his YouTube videos and controversial behavior. Paul has been involved in various controversies throughout his career and generally comes across as an obnoxious imbecile. His detour into boxing (fighting washed up UFC fighrers) was a rather sad commentary on how an idiot from YouTube can make more money from the sport than most real boxers. Jake Paul's real boxing ability was illustrated when he fought British reality television star and eight fight novice Tommy Fury. Fury outboxed Paul easily (despite a rather preposterous split decision verdict for Fury - who had won comfortably).

In March, 2024, it was announced that Mike Tyson would fight Jake Paul on Netflix at the AT&T Stadium in Arlington, Texas. The Texas Department of Licensing and Regulations confirmed the bout will be a sanctioned, professional fight. Mike Tyson was 58. Jake Paul was 27. Mike Tyson was reported to earning a purse of $20 million to fight Jake Paul. He hadn't had a payday that big since he fought Holyfield back in the 1990s.

Was the Tyson v Paul fight a scam? Is it a real fight? Has the result been scripted? Maybe it doesn't really matter. A sideshow circus attraction. The fight bore no relevance to Mike Tyson's boxing career - which effectively ended when he was destroyed by Lennox Lewis over twenty years ago. In fact, Tyson's real boxing career more or less ended in 1992 when he went to prison. He was never the same after prison - which is a shame. Had Tyson not gone to prison he would have fought Holyfield, Bowe, Lewis, and perhaps even Foreman in the early 1990s. Who knows what would have happened if he'd fought Holyfield and Lewis closer to his prime.

How good had Tyson been? The knock against Tyson was that his prime came in the 1980s - generally regarded to be a weak era for heavyweight boxing. It's a cliché but boxers can only fight the people they share their time with. Ali's legend was secured by the incredible supporting cast. Liston, Frazier, Foreman, Norton et al. It wasn't Tyson's fault that great heavyweights were thin on the ground in his prime. One could be pedantic and argue that Larry Holmes didn't have the greatest roster of challengers in his long reign. When Joe Louis made 25 defences of the heavyweight title his toil was often dubbed the "bum of the month club" because of the perceived weakness of many of his challengers. Rocky Marciano retired undefeated but he only made six defences of the heavyweight title and didn't stick around to fight Floyd Patterson. People often wonder if Wladimir Klitschko beat anyone of real note in his lengthy tenure as heavyweight champ. The point is not to discredit any of these men, all great fighters and champions, but merely to remember that boxers can only beat what is put in front of them.

It is difficult to rank Tyson because of the weird nature of his career - which had three acts. The third act (the post-prison act) tends to drag him down in historical lists due to his defeats to Holyfield. We should remember though that Tyson's absolute prime was 1986 to 1988. Think of the Tyson who beat Trevor Berbick or the Tyson who wiped out Michael Spinks. That version of Tyson would have been a danger to any fighter in history.

Has Tyson found peace at last? His life seems more placid and normal than anyone could have expected and he's managed to avoid the jail cell or early grave that many predicted would be his final destination. "This is a weird feeling in my life I have to deal with, not being a violent man anymore when my whole life's reputation was built on being extremely violent," said Tyson. "I just don't know how to deal with that right now. I don't even go to strip clubs no more. I don't know who

I am sometimes, but I am not the guy I used to be. I'm not an angel or anything. I'm still lascivious, periodically. I'm just looking for some balance in my life. I don't know that person anymore, that guy in '86, '87. I don't know that guy no more. I don't have no affinity for that guy no more. I have no affinity for the guy who said, 'I am the greatest fighter God produced.' I have no affinity for the guy who said he would try to push his (opponents) nose bone up into his brain. I just don't know that guy. I don't know who he is. I don't know where he came from. I don't have no kind of connection with him no more."

# Photo Credit

https://commons.wikimedia.org/wiki/File:Mike_Tyson_Phot
o_Op_GalaxyCon_Columbus_2023.jpg

2 December 2023,

Super Festivals